THE ROAD TO WEATHERFIELD

Barry Hill

Published by Paragon Publishing, Rothersthorpe
First published 2014

A catalogue record for this book is available from the British
Library.

ISBN 978-1-78222-324-5

Book design, layout and production management by Into Print
www.intoprint.net
+44 (0)1604 832149

Printed and bound in UK and USA by Lightning Source

ABOUT THE AUTHOR

Barry Hill was a member of the *Coronation Street* scriptwriting team for almost 30 years. Over that period he wrote some 300 episodes of the world's most successful drama serial.

He grew up in post-war Britain as the local rep and variety theatres were coming back into their heyday, when many of the stars who had entertained the troops during wartime and lifted the spirits of a flagging nation became more than a voice on the air waves. He didn't just witness the meteoric rise of live entertainment in those post-war years, but lived it passionately, which was ultimately to lead to his own first hand involvement as a member of the writing team of the most successful television drama serial in the world.

As well as writing for *Coronation Street*, he has also worked extensively in many other areas of press, television and radio.

His cruise ship lectures have covered anecdotes and behind-the-scenes tales from the golden years of rep and variety theatre, of soap opera in general and *Coronation Street* in particular.

His other books include *The Bits Between the Adverts*, a humorous account of life as a reporter on a weekly newspaper in a Cheshire town in the 1960s; *So You Want to be a Writer*, a comprehensive guide to writing for pleasure; and *Congratulations – You're a Senior Citizen*, a light-hearted guide to retirement.

.

THE ROAD TO WEATHERFIELD

AT THE BEGINNING of 2014, ITV Studios moved from its Quay Street studios in Manchester to purpose-built state of the art headquarters at Media City, Salford.

Granada Television, one of the pioneers of independent television broadcasting in this country, had occupied the Quay Street site for almost 60 years. From the launch of independent television in the mid-1950s, the company rapidly became a leading player in the broadcasting revolution which was to change our entertainment and viewing habits for ever.

Much has been written about *Coronation Street* since it was first transmitted into our living rooms. Many accolades and plaudits have been justifiably heaped on the programme, its creator Tony Warren, and the production teams and actors who had the courage to launch the show over five decades ago. And, over subsequent years, on those who have kept it at the top of the television ratings. The reason for this success is plain to see. Quite simply, since that very first episode, it has touched the hearts and minds of the nation.

I have been associated with GTV for almost half the time at Quay Street, for the most part as a scriptwriter for *Corrie,* which after more than five decades is still considered to be the greatest television show on earth.

Over the past six decades, enormous progress has been made in both technology and programme making. But during the previous six decades, from the dawn of the 20th century when music hall was at the height of its popularity, the entertainment scene underwent equally dramatic change as the major players of the day adapted to the new and exciting challenges that presented themselves.

In *The Road to Weatherfield* I take a look at the entertainment scene from the beginning of the 20th century when music hall reigned, at the world of the entertainers who made their name through radio and the gramophone, the wartime concert parties, the northern film scene and the golden era of variety and rep which reached a zenith as they raised the spirits and satisfied the demands of eager post-war audiences.

At the growth, influence and immeasurable contribution of the Granada group when all this rich heritage was drawn together to meet the challenge of changing times with the launch of ITV.

And my own experiences over almost three decades of writing for *Corrie,* getting the show on air from script to screen, and some of the unscheduled happenings behind the scenes along the way.

B.H.

To my dear wife, Avril, without whose ceaseless support and encouragement we would never have been able to live the dream. To Richard, Joanne, Max, Millie, Sarah and Oliver for just being there. To the staff at Salford Royal and The Christie hospitals, without whose skills and care I would not have been here to finish this book. And to the memory of those talented and creative folk I knew and worked with at Granada Television for almost three decades who are sadly no longer with us.

ACKNOWLEDGEMENTS

I WOULD LIKE to thank the many friends and colleagues who have shared their thoughts and memories with me in the writing of this book. Their skills and enthusiasm have contributed so much to making independent television what it is today.

The sources of my material have been wide and diverse. My aim has been to give a snapshot of the background to the entertainment business that led to the formation of ITV, and its relevance to the story I have set out to tell.

There are many enthusiasts with a lot more knowledge of their subjects than I, who have written in great depth about so many aspects of the entertainment business and the stars that I have only been able to touch on. I hope that this book will encourage readers to look further into the many works available. I can assure them that they will be more than adequately rewarded.

I would like to thank them all for recording and recounting in such detail what was to me a golden era of entertainment, for giving so many folk so much pleasure and for ensuring that those stars of days gone by are not forgotten.

CONTENTS

THE WRITER'S TALE 147

FOREWORD

THE TWO YOUNG mums were standing by a sparkling black 4 x 4 the size of a modest tank parked outside the school gates, brows furrowed as they voiced their concerns over their worsening financial situation.

'Heavens knows where it's all going to end,' said one.

'Wayne will have to come out of that school for a start,' came the response.

'And there's no chance of India going, now.'

Mrs (or was it Ms?) 4 x 4 shook her head in despair, as she unlocked the vehicle, prepared to climb aboard and retrace her route along the three hundred yards or so she had travelled from home.

Then, with a pert smile, financial crisis now dealt with: 'I'm meeting Cherie in Starbucks at eleven. If you're in the village.' Her friend nodded, invitation accepted.

'See you later.'

Conversation over.

But despair not, Wayne, India and the countless thousands like you. The credit crunch may have been threatening to herald the end of civilisation as some of you currently know it. But there is a glimmer of hope. Take heart.

Some of us have been there before – and we're still here to tell the tale.

When my sister and I were about the same age as Wayne and India, we travelled the mile or so to school each day in a different way, as so many other children still do today, though it would be a real novelty for some. It involves putting one foot in front of the other, transferring our body weight alternately from left to right, then repeating the process until we reach our destination.

I believe the technical name for it is walking.

If it was wet, it was a matter of on with the raincoat, on with the sou'wester, up with the umbrella, and – treat of treats – on with the wellies. If the weather was particularly bad, we may go part way on the bus, bright red with North Western Road Car Company emblazoned across its rump, a warm, dry refuge from the elements.

If we travelled further afield. we used the bus a lot. Or the train. They were the only means of transport available to us.

Not that we travelled far. We didn't have to. Most of our relatives lived fairly close. It was quite usual in those days for families to have stayed in the same area for generations. Been taught at the same school, worked at the same factory, even lived in the same house.

And when we left school to go home, we wouldn't be met at the school gate by mum animatedly chatting to half a dozen of her friends, waiting to shepherd us to the family limousine. We would walk back, where we would more likely than not find her hot, bothered and looking like a wrung-out dishcloth after spending all day doing the family washing.

There was no automatic washing machine. It was all done by hand in a big tub, which had been hauled within range of the sink in the kitchen for the day, before she painstakingly squeezed the water out of every item as she put it through the old mangle before hanging it out to dry.

We didn't have a dryer. If it was raining, the washing would be hanging from a ceiling rack in the kitchen, or draped over a clothes maiden in the front room.

One good thing about wash days, though, was that no matter how cold the weather outside, home was always warm from the steam, even though it was impossible to see through the windows because of the condensation.

On other days, it was a different story. We had no central heating. We did have a coal fire in the living room. The coal man delivered every two weeks, humping the sacks from his battered lorry to our back yard on his broad shoulders.

The fire had to be laboriously raked out and re-lit every day. This was usually left until late on, especially on a Monday which was traditionally washing day, or the smoky fire would have sprayed the newly-laundered garments hanging out to dry with thick globs of soot, as it joined with countless other coal fires to pollute the air outside to such a degree you could not only taste it every time you went out, but could practically cut it with a knife.

If we wanted to put on warm clothes on a bitterly freezing day, we had to hang them on the open oven door first.

Traditionally, every day of the week had a different function. Monday was washing day, Tuesday cleaning downstairs. Wednesday ironing, Thursday cleaning upstairs. Friday was reserved for the main shopping trip of the week, when we would collect and pay for the grocery order – no credit cards, strictly cash.

There were few colourful packets. Butter was cut from a large block and skilfully patted into a roughly rectangular shape before being wrapped in greaseproof paper. Cheese was cut by wire, for the most part with astonishing accuracy. Sugar was weighed out from a sack and served up in blue paper bags.

If anyone living alone wanted just two slices of bacon one egg and a tomato for tea, Mr Wright who ran the village grocer's shop was only too pleased to oblige. And if money was running a bit low towards the end of the week and you fancied a treat, there was always the broken biscuit tin with its variety of multi-coloured goodies at bargain prices.

We didn't have a freezer or a fridge, so food shopping wasn't a matter of nipping out to the supermarket at any time of the day or night, buying multi packs, stocking up with frozen pre-packed meals and feverishly snapping up the two-for-one offers, all stacked in attractive, colourful columns as far as the eye could see.

For bread, we went to the bakers, for fruit and vegetables to the greengrocers, for fish to the fishmongers, and for meat to the butchers. The milk man delivered every morning from his horse drawn trap, the milk either bottled or ladled straight from the churn into jugs. As we got older, as a treat at weekend we were allowed to help him with his deliveries, our reward being a ride back to the farm in the delivery trap at the end of the round.

For convenience, some folk were lucky enough, as we were, to have a nearby corner shop. It was run by a Mrs Croft and her sister, consisted of not much more than a garden shed, but had a seemingly inexhaustible stock of just about everything we ever seemed to need. Where they stored it all remains to this day one of life's unsolved mysteries.

Throw in the multitude of other domestic tasks, cleaning, pressing, sewing, mending, darning, altering clothes because we were very much children of the make-do-and-mend generation – in some homes it really was a case of first up, best dressed – and the fact that the majority of mums had a job of some sort as well, not to pay for their timeshare in Tenerife but to help to put food on the table, there were times when you wondered how many of them ever found time to go to bed.

Yet I remember quite vividly one aspect of family life as a youngster. We almost always found time to sit down together once a day for a proper meal, the preparation of which was one more task for the hard-pressed matriarch of the family.

Occasionally, as a special treat, we would go to the local takeaway – the fish and chip shop. That was all there was in those days. How on earth we managed to survive without Italian, Chinese, Japanese, Indian, Thai, Turkish, Greek, Lebanese and the hundred and one other gastronomic delights on offer today, we'll never know. The nearest we came to international cuisine was when Idris Roberts and his wife moved into our village from north Wales to take over the chip shop.

But on the positive side, we never had to worry whether a decent claret, a smooth chardonnay or a piquant rose would go best with fish, chips and Manchester caviar, known more universally as mushy peas. Which was just as well. Wine was something that hadn't even entered our vocabulary, let alone our world.

The only time we had alcohol in our house was when dad had one of his pals round and he would get in a couple of bottles of pale ale from the off licence.

Which was a further highlight in our young lives, as we were allowed to take the empty bottles back and claim the penny deposit on them for ourselves. It couldn't be called recycling. That hadn't been invented then.

School wasn't the pleasant, warm, friendly welcoming place that it can be today, either.

There was no heating in the classrooms. The big assembly hall in winter was probably the coldest spot in the northern hemisphere. Teachers were strict. We spent most of the day at our desks, apart from the brief taste of freedom at playtime and lunchtime. And while we were in school, what the teachers said was law. No arguments. We had no choice in the matter. We didn't have the option of running to the European Court of Human Rights.

Just as we respected the teachers, we respected the law, other people's property, and their right to live their lives without any interference from us. If we didn't, we would have been faced with the ultimate penalty – being marched home by the local bobby to be dealt with by an irate parent, not only for the misdemeanour that had attracted the attention of the law, but for bringing such disgrace on the family.

We didn't rush home from school to watch TV. We didn't have TV. It would be several more years before we did, then it was only the one BBC station. Broadcast entertainment to us was listening to the wireless – either the Home Service or the Light Programme.

We didn't have computers. To us, the world wide web was something that would have been created in a science fiction film by an invasion of giant spiders.

We didn't have WiFi, Play Stations, DVD recorders, CD players, MP3s or IPhones. Tablets were medication prescribed by the doctor when you were ill.

We didn't contact friends through our webcam, or phone them or text them every few seconds on our mobiles. We didn't phone them full stop. Because we didn't have a telephone of any kind for some time, then when we did eventually have one installed it was a shared line – we could only make a call when the other party wasn't using it.

We didn't have mountain bikes or quad bikes. We would make bogey trucks out of old pram wheels and a couple of planks of wood.

The more fortunate of us may have access to a second hand bike, usually too small or too big, but fully functional. You could easily pick out the posher kids. Their bikes had been slicked up with a coat of paint, choice of colour never being an issue as the paint was usually left over from decorating the living room. And it would probably sport newly-fashioned handle grips made out of war surplus gas mask tubing.

Those of us lucky to have access to a bike who had dreams of sitting astride the petrol tank of a Norton 500 motor cycle, would fold a cardboard cigarette packet and jam it behind the front brake block so that the spokes struck it every time the wheel revolved, making a sound like a rapid-fire machine gun which gave us a passable impression of a Norton 500 motorbike.

Most toys were second hand, or made by well-meaning relatives. But it never bothered us. In the main, we made our own amusement, anyway. We didn't need sports centres or designated playing fields. If there weren't two willing souls to turn a rope, usually a length of discarded washing line, while the third one skipped, two could manage just as well. They would simply tie one end of the rope to a convenient drain pipe or lamp post – ready-to-hand supports of which we made full use.

The washing line would also come in handy on occasion when we needed to tie up the dog to stop him running off with the ball, or to dish out some form of summary punishment for a minor misdemeanour committed by one of the gang.

He or she would be lashed to the lamp post until tea time, the miscreant always hoping that we would remember to release them before we went home.

A major misdemeanor was dealt with by instant expulsion.

The same lamp post would also come into its own when the lads needed to show off their super-human strength by hanging from the cross bar near the top by their arms until the aching became too much to bear, or when we played cricket using the base for stumps.

And when we were out, we were out. We walked. No arguing. No third umpire.

When it came to football, who needed replica shirts? We didn't even need goal posts. Two coats placed on the ground, and you were set for the day. Granted, it wasn't a perfect arrangement, with constant claims that it was over the bar or over the post, neither of which actually existed. But we would accept the general consensus of opinion and just get on with the game.

There were no equality laws in those days. Lads were lads and girls were girls. But above all, we were all kids together.

During the summer months, we would spend hours rolling marbles along the dusty gutters at the side of the road, unimpeded by endless rows of parked cars. Or playing hop scotch on the pavement. Or flicking cardboard milk bottle tops against the wall to see who could get the nearest, winner taking all.

We were a generation of avid collectors. We would sit for hours trading cigarette cards, discarded cigarette packets, windfall fruit (much of which needed a bit of help falling from the trees) – in fact anything that was collectible.

When autumn came, we collected conkers and fought endless battles with them to see who was the champion for that year, amid grave accusations of dirty tricks, such as soaking the smooth, shiny chestnuts in vinegar or baking them in the oven to make them invincible.

A sheet thrown over a clothes maiden made a passable tent, holiday home, theatre or shop. Or we would put the Morrison shelter left over from the war years that took up most of our living room to similar practical use.

Occasionally, we would put our dog or next door's cat underneath, held captive by the wire mesh sides, and boast that we had saved the world from the threat of a rampant wild beast running free and terrorising civilisation.

And when the shelter, originally installed to protect us from air raids, wasn't being used to satisfy our imaginative flights of fantasy, its cold, flat surface was transformed into a more than passable dining room table.

During the dark evenings of winter, we would play board games, read, make model aeroplanes, listen to the wireless or just use our imagination. My first foray into the world of entertainment was when I built a radio station from bits and pieces from the war surplus shop to serve the uninvited and for the most part unrequired entertainment needs of friends and family.

The microphones had previously seen service in wartime fighter planes. What a tale they could have told.

The local war surplus shop was a veritable treasure house to many a lad with imagination and a will to make something useful from odds and ends that could be picked up there.

I had two cousins who actually made television receivers of sorts out of parts picked up in war surplus shops. The screens were no bigger than a postcard, and the cabinet was the size of a modest wardrobe, but undeniably they were capable of picking up pictures and sound – though not always necessarily at the same time.

Foreign holidays, air travel – long distance travel of any kind – had no place in our lives. If we did manage a family holiday, it was usually to the nearest seaside. Not to a resort centre, country club or health spa offering a range of treatments and activities, or timeshare on some sun-drenched exotic island, but to a modest semi in Cleveleys or Prestatyn, run as holiday digs by Mrs Burkinshaw or Mrs Owen. And then just for a week at most.

A la carte and table d'hote were as foreign to us as the country where the terms originated. More often than not we took our own food in a cardboard box, for the landlady to cook (the food, not the cardboard box, though on occasion it would be difficult to tell the difference). If we wanted condiments provided with our meal, it was usually clearly stated that use of cruet was extra.

This was due in no small part to post-war rationing, of course, which was of greater concern to our parents than to us youngsters, and it was only many years later that we really appreciated the massive effort and planning they had put into ensuring that we had a few days by the sea.

But we still managed to enjoy ourselves. And grow into adulthood.

I'm not suggesting for one minute that the way forward is to rip out the central heating, throw out the washing machines, freezers, TV sets, computers and mobile phones.

Of course, we are so much better off today in a multitude of ways – longer life expectancy, better education, superb communications and generally better opportunities for the fulfilment of so many.

When I look at my grandchildren I can't help reflecting on those days of my own childhood and recalling how little our families had by comparison. Or did we?

We learned to have respect for others and for authority, to take responsibility for our own actions, to take pleasure in simple things, to value the rewards of success and to cope with despair and failure when it beset our lives. And to be there for others.

We built relationships based on true friendship and trust, not on how impressed we were with someone else's image on their social website.

And we went on to produce some of the most brilliant businessmen, scientists, innovative thinkers and life-changing inventions of the last two thousand years.

We even managed to produce a World Cup-winning football team!

And we were entertained by some of the finest variety turns and actors performing on radio, in theatres and in end-of-pier shows throughout the country, their skills honed on the necessity to lift the spirits of a nation ravaged by wartime.

We were witness to the development of commercial television as a mainstream source of entertainment, which was to bring us what I and many others will always consider to be the greatest show on earth, *Coronation Street* – that incredible, durable creation by Tony Warren that was to became such a major part of so many people's lives for generations to come, and was to become a massive part of mine for almost 30 years.

I have been very proud and privileged to be associated with such an icon of television entertainment, to share so many moments of magic and memories with some of the finest entertainers of their generation who brought so much pleasure to so many people and brought so much colour and happiness into the lives of myself and my family.

In this book I have set out to record one of the most innovative periods in the history of British show business and the years leading up to it – the boom years for countless variety turns and rep actors during the decade following the second world war, the ultimate demise of many of them as theatres brought down the curtain for the last time during the 1950s, and their rise again as they found themselves standing on the threshold of an exciting new form of family entertainment – commercial television.

What was for me, as a *Coronation Street* scriptwriter for almost three decades, and for so many others, truly a golden age.

CHANGING TIMES

1

THE GOOD OLD DAYS

THE TRADITION OF music hall is believed to have had its origins in London at the beginning of the 19th century. By the 1830s it had become firmly established, as the new style concert rooms and saloon bars in public houses flourished. By the turn of the century, just about every town in Britain had a music hall.

Featuring a mixture of popular song, comedy and speciality acts, the intention of the song and supper rooms was to attract folk in to be entertained and thus increase the sales of alcohol. An admission fee was usually charged, or the bar prices were higher.

Consequently the song and supper rooms tended initially to attract the more wealthy people, but as the working classes began to see a reduction in working hours giving them more leisure time, they too became regular visitors, even though many of them could ill afford it.

One of the most famous London meeting places at that time was the Grecian Saloon at the Eagle on the City Road, a former tea garden, which was thought by many to have inspired the second verse of the nursery rhyme *Pop Goes the Weasel.*

Up and down the City Road,
In and out the Eagle.
That's the way the money goes,
Pop goes the Weasel.

Weasel was an abbreviated corruption of whistle and flute, cockney rhyming slang for suit, the implication being that it would be pawned weekly in order to get the money to spend in the Eagle.

Many guardians of human morality of the time were far from approving of the rapid growth in popularity of the song and supper rooms, and the way in which the local low life and ladies of easy virtue preyed on the customers was heavily condemned by many.

But the newly-emerging venues proved to be very popular with punters and performers alike – particularly with the artistes. Many who got their first taste of entertaining an audience in the song and supper rooms went on to become big stars, some barely into their teens when they took their first steps into the big world of music hall. Marie Lloyd was just 14 when she made her debut at the Grecian Saloon.

Despite disapproval and opposition from some quarters, music hall continued to thrive as a popular form of entertainment, the song and supper rooms eventually being eclipsed by the growing number of variety theatres, which were to soar in popularity following the first world war as they provided the feast of entertainment that a war-weary nation was desperate for.

One of the major influences in the soaring popularity of the variety theatres during those post war years was undoubtedly the advent of radio broadcasting.

The first radio broadcast from London was on 14th November 1922 and it was made by the British Broadcasting Company which had been formed earlier that year when the government licensed six major radio manufacturers to run the operation.

The British Broadcasting Corporation was formed some four years later in 1926 by Royal charter, following its coverage of the national strike. John Reith, who had been the founding managing director of the commercial company, became the first Director of the new BBC.

Radio broadcasting was to do for many acts what television was to do following the second world war – to bring the comics, the musicians, the singers, the impressionists, the speciality acts to a nationwide audience.

Artistes who had worked the music halls and theatres for years and may never have been heard of outside the north of England, or London, or wherever they happened to concentrate their work, could become overnight national treasures through radio. And there was no doubt at all that a radio appearance could prove the key to box office success.

Before the advent of the BBC, there were other ways performers, especially musicians, could be more widely heard, particularly by the better off.

In 1877, Thomas Edison invented the tinfoil phonograph, which played recorded sounds from round tinfoil cylinders. The sound quality was poor and they could be played only once. But it was the launching pad for further work in the field, and Edison's invention was followed by Alexander Graham Bell's graphophone, which used wax cylinders that could be played many times.

While being a big improvement on Edison's invention, Bell's graphophone was not the perfect way of bringing recordings within reach of the general public. Each cylinder had to be recorded separately. There was no way of mass producing them.

But all that was to change in 1887, when Emile Berliner, a German immigrant living and working in Washington, USA, invented the gramophone, a system of sound recording that recorded on flat discs, initially made of glass, then zinc and eventually of plastic. More importantly the recordings could be replayed and mass produced from masters.

The commercial recording era which was to create national and eventually international stars had arrived.

But it was undoubtedly the advent of radio that was responsible for bringing entertainment to mass audiences on a grand scale.

One of the most popular and best known music halls in the north of England in the latter part of the 19th century was not only to defy the trend when others were eventually bringing down the curtain for the last time, but is in fact still going strong today. The City Varieties in Leeds, built in 1865, is one of the rare surviving examples of Victorian music hall.

Founded by local pub landlord and benefactor Charles Thornton and adjoining the White Swan Inn, it was known initially as Thornton's Music Hall and Fashion Lounge, before becoming White Swan Varieties, Stansfield Varieties and eventually the City Palace of Varieties.

In 1953, BBC producer Barney Colehan made a television programme from the theatre in which he recreated the era of old time music hall, with acts performing and audience dressed appropriately to the period.

The Good Old Days proved to be such a hit with viewers that it was to run for another 30 years, not only recreating the spirit of Victorian music hall but providing new opportunities for many variety artistes, both established acts and newcomers to the business.

And thanks to a recently-completed £9.9m programme of refurbishment, the story of the City Varieties goes on, set to continue its proud heritage as one of the leading theatrical venues in the country.

2

FROM SILVER SCREEN TO SMALL SCREEN

THERE IS ABSOLUTELY no doubt in the mind of anyone who knew him, that the driving force behind Granada Television was Sidney Bernstein.

Sidney Lewis Bernstein was born in Ilford Essex in 1899. He left school at the age of 15. Some seven years later, together with brother Cecil, he inherited a small chain of cinemas in southern England from his father. And during their lifetime the brothers went on to become two of the most influential men in the entertainment business.

Sidney and Cecil, with the help of younger brothers Albert and Max, built up that initial small chain into a circuit of some 60 cinemas and theatres. They named it Granada Theatres Ltd after a favourite spot of Sidney's in Spain.

As the Granada chain of cinemas and theatres flourished, so too did the wider range of Granada influence, which was eventually to go on to embrace a whole string of companies in the leisure industry, including not only cinema and theatre, but also television, bowling alleys, motorway services, publishing and a television rental business.

But it was film and eventually television that remained the abiding passion of Sidney, and it was initially in the film industry that he continued to make his name. He was not only ever-sensitive to the changing mood for popular entertainment and adept at keeping abreast of public demand, but he also led the way in innovation. The introduction of Saturday morning matinees for children is one example.

At the outbreak of the second world war, Sidney Bernstein, who was a founding member of the British Film Society, was chairman of the Granada Group. His expertise, experience and overall knowledge of the entertainment scene was put to immediate use and during the following years he had a number of highly influential roles.

He was appointed film adviser to the British Ministry of Information, two years later being posted to the British Embassy in Washington D.C. in a similar capacity. That same year he was named Chief of the Film Section, Allied Forces in North Africa, and a year later, Chief of the Film Section, Allied Forces in Europe. He also served under General Eisenhower as Chief of the Film Section at Supreme Headquarters Allied Expedition Forces (SHAEF).

His mission with all these appointments was to lift the morale of the troops, which he undoubtedly did through the production of his many films.

After the war, in 1948, Sidney joined forces with his friend film director Alfred Hitchcock to form their own film production company, Transatlantic Pictures.

The Granada Theatres chain continued to expand as Sidney and Cecil Bernstein kept abreast of changing moods and public taste, and when in 1954 the Television Act was passed, which would end the monopoly of the BBC and give private companies a right to apply for broadcasting franchises on a regional basis, the brothers were ready and eager to rise to the new challenge.

They applied for the franchise for the north of England, which surprised many who thought they may have gone for a region nearer the south. But they were looking for an area where they could create a strong regional identity and where their television interests would not be too detrimental to their cinema operation, which was largely southern based.

And the north of England was appealing for many reasons.

Not only would it provide an opportunity to establish new creative industry outside the capital, but the region – and Manchester in particular – had a strong history of home grown cultural development in literature, newspapers, theatre and music.

It was the home of the Manchester Guardian newspaper, the Halle Orchestra and had seen the emergence of the first repertory company under the direction of Miss Annie Horniman. And there was a wealth of entertainment talent, many star names having contributed much to the success of Mancunian Films.

The newly-formed Granada Television was awarded the franchise to broadcast in the north of England from Monday to Friday. The weekend franchise went to ABC Television, which belonged to Associated British Picture Corporation.

On 3rd May 1956, Granada Television started transmission in Lancashire, but it was to be another six months before they could transmit programmes in Yorkshire. The reason for this was that two new transmitters had to be built, one at Winter Hill in Lancashire, and one at Emley Moor in Yorkshire. And while the Winter Hill transmitter was up and running by May, its Yorkshire counterpart would not be ready until November.

Sidney and Cecil's belief in their ability to extend their cinema expertise into the brave new world of television quickly proved well founded. By January 1957, Granada Television was credited with the top ten programmes in the region, and quickly established a reputation as one of the leading independent television contractors.

Two years later, Alex Bernstein, son of Cecil joined the Granada Group, and in due course he was to take on many of the top roles in the company, including variously joint managing director, deputy chairman and eventually chairman.

Alex had a keen interest in theatre and the arts, reflected in the many roles he took on alongside his work with the Granada Group, which included the chairmanship of Manchester's Royal Exchange Theatre and the Old Vic in London. He received recognition for his work in 2000 when he became a Life Peer.

The company was to receive great acclaim for its high-profile current affairs, news and documentary programmes such as *World in Action, Disappearing World* and *Seven Up*. The Beatles made their first TV appearance in 1962 from the company's Quay Street studios. The first General Election debate to be held on ITV came from there, too. The Granada Group was to become one of the biggest and most powerful entertainment empires in the country, while the television operation went from strength to strength with its diverse programme output.

Sidney Bernstein, was a man of many facets, but always primarily an unashamed showman. Throughout the Granada studios complex in Manchester, he liberally displayed posters of one of his greatest influences, Phineas T Barnum, of Barnum and Bailey circus fame. The posters for the circus, billed as the greatest show on earth, were a constant reminder to staff that the role of Granada Television was to make the greatest television shows on earth.

And in *Coronation Street*, Sidney's company had arguably achieved exactly that.

He was a man of strong ideals who will be forever remembered for his colossal contribution to the 20th century entertainment scene, which was recognised in 1969 when he was created a Life Peer.

One of Sidney Bernstain's proudest moments came in 1984 when he received the recognition he so richly deserved for his contribution to the film industry where his career had started when he was named a Fellow of the British Film Institute.

When Sidney stood down as chairman of Granada Television, it was to herald the start of a partnership that not only dominated the Granada Television operation for the next two decades, but was one of the most powerful in the television industry.

It was to bring together Denis Forman, who succeeded Sidney as chairman, and programme controller David Plowright.

Denis Forman, who had been one of the founding executives of Granada TV in the 1950s, became joint managing director some 10 years later and following Sidney's retirement from the position became chairman. He was also chairman of the Granada Group for many years, and his interests and influence in the arts were many and diverse, particularly in the field of music. He was awarded an OBE in recognition of his work at about the time that ITV was taking to the air, and in 1976 he was honoured with a knighthood.

David Plowright was a programme maker, who had already made his mark in television broadcasting when Denis Forman took over as chairman. As programme controller he had been responsible for the airing of some of the most innovative drama and cutting edge documentary programme-making in television. In 1975 he became managing director and eventually chairman of GTV until his retirement in 1992.

Sir Denis Foreman and David Plowright were to drive Granada Television to even greater heights bringing their influence and experience to bear on producing a stream of outstanding quality programming, particularly evident in the company's drama output which received unsurpassed viewer and critical acclaim with productions including *A Family at War*, *Lost Empires*, *Brideshead Revisited* and *Jewel in the Crown*.

I am delighted to have worked with Sir Denis Forman and David Plowright, and privileged to have known Sidney Bernstein, and in my own way, minute as it may have been in the overall scheme of things, to have contributed to perpetuating his dream.

3

AS ONE DOOR CLOSES . . .

THE FIRST EPISODE of *Coronation Street,* the world's most successful television drama serial, was transmitted at 7.00pm on Friday, 9th December 1960.

ITV had started broadcasting in the north of England in May 1956, twenty years after the launch of BBC television in 1936 and some four years before the first episode of *Coronation Street* was launched from the studios of Granada Television in Manchester.

But the arrival of commercial television on the entertainment scene was not initially celebrated by everyone. Many people 'in the business' saw the outlook only as bleak, fearing the launch of ITV would herald the death knell for countless local rep companies and variety theatres up and down the country.

For those who had earned a respectable living in these venues for so many years, the future certainly didn't look too bright anyway as so many theatres at this time were already disappearing quicker than bathwater down the plughole. Many had been built before the turn of the century and were in urgent need of refurbishment, for which there wasn't the cash available.

In 1956, I was 19 years old and doing my National Service in the Royal Navy. Before I went away, Saturday night entertainment for me was either the radio, the cinema, the local dance hall, repertory theatre or a variety show in Manchester.

But when I returned, things were certainly different. The

entertainment scene as I had known it was changing beyond recognition.

Viewers previously had only BBC television to watch. When the newly-hatched ITV shook out its feathers, flexed its wings and took its first tentative flight of fantasy into our lives through the box in the corner of our living room, viewers had a wider choice of entertainment than they had ever had before – and all at the touch of a button and without leaving the comfort of their armchairs.

And by 1960, when the strains of that haunting *Coronation Street* signature tune first took to the air, commercial television was very much a major part of our lives.

So why did our twice-weekly visits to the cobbled streets of Weatherfield have such an impact on viewing audiences from the very first episode?

Well obviously the creator, Tony Warren, had got the formula exactly right. The characters were finely drawn, viewers could instantly identify with them and the creative team at Granada Television did the rest. The setting was realistic, the writing, acting, production values were to the highest standard – and the time was right.

Theatre was changing. The gritty reality of the working classes, was making an impact. To me, there were probably two productions that epitomised the changing scene. John Osborne's *Look Back in Anger* had first been produced in 1956, followed two years later by the film version. That same year, Joan Littlewood staged the first performance of Shelagh Delaney's *A Taste of Honey* at Stratford East, which was also to reach a much wider audience, when it, too, was brought to the cinema screen.

Undoubtedly, there was not only an interest in but an appetite for drama based on the stark reality of the working classes. If it worked in the theatre and in the cinema, why not on television? The time was ripe for an ongoing drama made for the small screen about real life, real people in very real situations.

It was out of this climate that *Coronation Street* was born, as Tony Warren skilfully wove the fabric that was to form the basis of the opening episodes and fought tooth and nail to bring his work to fruition. Initially, it wasn't seen as the way forward by every television executive, notably Sidney and Cecil Bernstein. But there was no way Tony was going to give up without a fight, and with the support of producer Harry Elton and director Derek Bennett he eventually triumphed and so placed an indelible stamp on television history.

And so the task of bringing the concept to the screen got underway. It was scheduled initially for thirteen episodes, and it was strongly felt that if it was going to work, the audience would have to be convinced that they were eavesdropping on reality.

So although there had been successful television drama series before the launch of *Coronation Street* – many of them produced in the north by Granada Television – and there were a number of fine actors already known to the casting directors, the programme makers decided initially to look for faces that were largely unknown to TV audiences.

It was felt that this would add to the gritty realism they wished to portray in the programme. That unknown faces would more readily be accepted as the characters they were playing than well-known established actors who had already made their mark in other television productions.

It was for the same reason, to ensure total acceptance by the viewers that the characters and events they were watching on screen were real and an extension to their own lives, that there were no repeats of *Coronation Street* for many years, to reinforce that feeling of reality, to ensure that the twice-weekly visits as they were then were a window onto a real parallel world.

As Sidney Bernstein said: 'There are no repeats in real life.'

For those actors who successfully auditioned for the initial running parts in the serial as well as for the increasing number of other drama productions that were being developed, and for those countless others who were to follow them, it could not have come at a better time, as many of the smaller regional theatres were closing their doors for the last time.

Not all of them, of course. Many repertory theatres, predominantly in the large towns and cities, and to a lesser degree in seaside resorts, particularly in the summer months, continued to flourish and are still very much alive today, where support is undiminished as the companies continually perform a wide variety of plays of all genre to the highest standards, producing and featuring some of the finest actors, as well as the most innovative directors and writers in modern day theatre.

But for many actors and performers who had earned a living in the regional variety theatres and local small town rep companies that were so much the hub of entertainment to family audiences during the years following the second world war, the future was looking none too rosy.

Sale Palace Theatre in Cheshire, home of my local rep, was a prime example. After years of producing a weekly and varied change of programme for the enjoyment of its loyal audience, the final curtain eventually came down on the company we had come to regard almost as members of our own family. Even as a theatre club, when the audience became 'members' providing a certain guarantee of a regular following, it was no longer financially viable.

It wasn't the first time that the building had changed direction. A decade earlier it had also been a favourite haunt of mine and my mates with its weekly offering of Saturday morning films, where we were first introduced to the celluloid heroes whose memory was to stay with us for life – Flash Gordon, Roy Rogers, Gene Autrey and their ilk.

This time, though, there was nowhere to go. When the curtain came down on the Sale Palace Players for the last time, it was the end of the road not only for the company but not long after for the theatre itself.

And it wasn't only the number of rep theatres that were in decline. Variety theatres, too, many with a long and proud history, were disappearing fast. By the mid-1950s there were only half the number of theatres in the country that there had been during their peak in the years before the second world war.

Manchester Hippodrome had provided my introduction to live variety theatre. On many a Saturday night I had seen some of the biggest names in the business, stars of radio who had almost overnight taken on a real flesh and blood existence to their many fans who had grown up with their acts over the air waves. It was a sad day when it, too, closed its doors for the last time.

Manchester's own film production company, Mancunian Films, which had brought so much northern talent to the silver screen after being launched in London, before opening studios in Manchester in a disused church in 1947, sold the premises to the BBC just seven years later.

The company had moved out of the city to continue production back in London where it had all started, albeit leaving a lasting legacy. Many of the company's technical staff as well as a wealth of entertainment talent who through the company's productions had become national favourites, went on to take their expertise into commercial television.

Times were changing. It wasn't all down to the advent of ITV, but undoubtedly it did accelerate the process.

But as one door closes another one opens, so the saying goes. Or to be more precise as one curtain came down for the last time, another one was beginning to rise. ITV, far from being the threat that so many initially feared, was to become the saviour of numerous careers.

And no more so than *Coronation Street*.

The staff both behind and in front of the cameras had joined the fledgling ITV companies from a variety of backgrounds – from Mancunian Films, from the BBC, from overseas television, from films, the theatre, amateur dramatics groups – and so the list goes on.

There were actors, journalists, presenters, writers, producers, directors, floor managers, cameramen, sound engineers, lighting technicians, electricians, designers, wardrobe mistresses, casting directors, props, secretaries, PAs. continuity staff, the list was seemingly endless, all ready, willing and eager to rise to the new challenge of the world of commercial television.

The conception, birth, development and progress of *Corrie*, as it is affectionately known, has been well documented over the years. As have the contributions made by the many actors who have been connected with the show, and who have gone down in television history, and quite rightly so, for the massive contribution they have made to the entertainment scene generally over the decades that it has been such a major part of our lives.

But many of them did have a life before independent television hit the air waves. For the majority, a life that was very different to that which was to bring them national fame and recognition after just one appearance on the small screen.

So what was it like to work for a small town weekly repertory company where, on a bad night, the small cast could outnumber the audience?

Where did the variety 'turns' find their material?

What was it like to be staying in digs where the only way the landlady knew how to cook a fillet steak was to boil it?

When for so many, nationwide fame and fortune was something that happened to someone else.

Until they found themselves, as I did, on the road to Weatherfield.

THE ACTOR'S TALE

4

ANNIE HORNIMAN –
FIRST LADY OF REP

ONE OF THE great pleasures for me over my many years working for *Coronation Street*, having been brought up under the influence of radio, rep theatre and variety theatre, has been the sheer joy of working with members of the cast who came from these backgrounds.

Those who came from a variety background would frequently refer to the actors as 'lahdies' – lahdie da, nose in the air. Saw themselves as superior. While actors would refer to the variety artistes as 'turns'.

This concept of 'us and them' was even taken up by the landladies in some of the digs where the performers stayed. There was an automatic assumption that tastes in food and home comforts were definitely more sophisticated when an 'actor' was staying there. There were some landladies who would go as far as having different crockery and bedding for their actors and turns – and tales of one landlady who didn't even bother to put cloths on the table for the variety folk!

It is indeed fitting that so many actors who have trod those famous cobbles of Weatherfield over the years have had a background in rep with companies in and around Manchester, for it was in that city that the concept of rep in this country was first launched in 1907 when Annie Horniman's company offered a repertoire of plays at the Midland Hotel in Manchester.

It proved to be a big success, and in 1908, the tea heiress, who had previously financed plays at the Avenue Theatre in London, and funded the opening of the Abbey Theatre in

Dublin, took over the Gaiety Theatre in Manchester which was to become her company's permanent home.

When the Gaiety was transformed into the Manchester Playgoers Theatre, it not only established the former touring venue as the first repertory theatre in the country, but ensured that Annie Horniman became a legend in the history of English theatre.

Annie Elizabeth Fredericka Horniman was born in Lewisham on October 3rd 1860, the eldest child of Frederick and Rebekah Horniman.

The family were not without substance. Her grandfather, John Horniman, had founded the family tea business. His idea of selling tea in packets of a guaranteed weight and purity was to make his fortune.

Annie's father had followed John Horniman into the family business, and during his extensive travels around the world on behalf of the company, he amassed a vast collection of curios, objets d'art and specimens of flora and fauna which was to form the basis of the Horniman Free Museum, which he set up at the family home in Forest Hill.

Family life strongly reflected their Victorian middle class background, and Annie and her brother Emslie endured a very strict upbringing. They never went to school, but were taught at home by private tutors and governesses. It was not until a German governess was appointed to look after the young Horniman children when Annie was barely a teenager that she and Emslie began to see that life had more to offer than they had hitherto ever dreamed of.

The German governess was a great fan of the provincial theatre movement in her homeland, and was keen to share her love of the theatre with her two young charges.

Unfortunately, in the eyes of a strict Victorian family, the theatre was not the kind of place where decent folk spent their time, any more than they would have indulged in card games, or, heaven forbid, smoking.

But the governess wanted to share her experiences and appreciation of the theatre with her two young charges, so shortly after Annie's thirteenth birthday, she felt the time was ripe to introduce the children to the delights of live performance.

Unbeknown to their parents, the governess took the children to see *The Merchant of Venice* at the Crystal Palace in London. It turned out to be one of the most memorable experiences they had had in their short lives, and on Annie in particular, it made a profound and lasting impression.

It was to fire within her a passionate love affair with the theatre that was to last a lifetime – an affair that was to drive her to establishing 35 years later in Manchester that company of actors that was to spearhead the repertory theatre movement in this country.

Although the Horniman children could not go to the theatre as much as they may have wished, and certainly not at all with their parents' knowledge, after that memorable first trip and in the privacy of their own quarters they pursued their latest interest in other ways under the watchful eye and encouragement of their beloved governess.

They would frequently build model theatres of their own, write their own plays, and make all the characters and costumes so they could act out their work.

But it was only a matter of time before the children could openly pursue their enthusiasm for the theatre, as attitudes became more liberal and many things that were considered unacceptable in 1874 were accepted with good grace, even acclaimed, some four or five years later.

By 1879 it had actually become fashionable to patronise the theatre, and when Annie went to see the visiting *Comedie*

Francaise, it was at least with her parents' permission, if not with their total approval.

She would probably have gone quite openly anyway. Young Annie's passionate interest in the theatre was not the only issue on which her views conflicted with those of her parents.

By now she had her own suite of rooms in the family home, and even her mother couldn't enter without being invited by Annie. And on the rare occasions on which she was allowed in, she despaired of what she saw.

What Annie wanted to do, she did, regardless of whether it was fitting for a young lady of considerable means or not, whether it was her endless practising of dance steps to feed her passion for dancing, or more to her mother's disgust, her smoking habit and the way she dressed, which could only be described as flamboyant.

Despite her mother's best efforts to get her to change her ways, any attempt to get Annie to dress and behave more in keeping with her family's expectations and her social position failed miserably. As well as smoking heavily, she dressed even more eccentrically and loved unusual jewellery.

There was indeed no shortage of money for the fineries that Mr and Mrs Horniman wished to shower on their daughter. Her father was by now head of the family tea business. But Annie continued to spurn the fine lifestyle that could have been hers for the asking.

As far as she was concerned, she had all the clothes she needed. If her mother didn't approve, that was her problem. Annie was happy the way she was and that was that.

And this was not the only way she rebelled against her parents and the Victorian middle class values and prejudices they represented. She ardently believed in the equality of the sexes and strongly supported the women's suffrage movement.

She also developed a well-informed interest in the occult and astrology.

She turned her back completely on the fine social life a young lady of her standing may have been expected to follow and in 1882 at the age of 22 she enrolled at London's Slade School of Art, where she was to stay for four years.

She didn't display any great artistic talent while she was there, but she was greatly influenced by many of the acquaintances she met, many of whom were to become leading figures in literature and drama.

She developed a love of continental travel, often going long distances with her bicycle alone. Inevitably, she was soon to make a trip to the country that she had heard so much about as a child from her governess. A country which was to captivate her – Germany.

Her first trip to Germany was to the Wagner festival, a pilgrimage she was to make many more times.

And while she was in Germany she had the opportunity to see for herself the work of the subsidised theatres and how they had become so much a cultural part of the communities they served. She also saw her first Ibsen play. She was so impressed with his work, with his exploration of contemporary social and psychological problems, that when she returned to England she was fired with a new passion for the theatre.

She had also become aware of the cultural values of the subsidised repertory theatres that were so numerous in Germany at that time, and in her determination to promote this drama at home, she joined the Independent Theatre Society.

Annie had for many years taken a deep interest in the occult, and round about this time she became deeply involved with a secret occult society, the Order of the Golden Dawn.

Through this connection, she was to meet many more influential people in the world of literature and drama – among them playwright W B Yeats and London stage actress and musician Florence Farr, both of whom were to become close friends and confidantes of Annie.

She was to remain a member of the Order until 1903, although during the latter years there was growing acrimony among the leading figures within the movement, which led ultimately to the resignations of both Yeats and Annie Horniman.

In 1893, Annie's grandfather died, and the legacy she was left heralded a new-found freedom. A freedom to live her own life as she wished and the opportunity to fund her first theatrical venture.

Her great friend Florence Farr was planning a new season of experimental drama at the Avenue Theatre in London, and Annie stepped in with the financial backing needed, despite the risks. She had long decided that many things she considered worthwhile had an element of risk. This only made them more exciting and appealing to her.

Unfortunately, Annie's enthusiasm for the venture wasn't reflected at the box office, and the season was not a financial success although it was critically acclaimed. Annie herself referred to it as a fruitful failure.

But it was notable in two respects. It gave a first public performance to *Arms and the Man*, the first play by George Bernard Shaw to be seen in the commercial theatre; and to *The Land of Heart's Desire,* the first play by W B Yeats to be performed in London.

And it was to herald a new era in the young Annie's life as her relationship with Yeats deepened.

Annie was delighted to have the acquaintance of a fine playwright. Yeats found Annie to be supportive, amusing and generally excellent company. Annie's offer of assistance in handling Yeats' personal business matters, including dealing with his correspondence and other work of a secretarial nature, was initially not taken seriously by Yeats. While he could certainly use such assistance, he felt he could not afford such an offer. How would a comparatively struggling writer such as himself be able to pay for the services of such a well-educated woman?

But Annie assured him that there would be no question of payment. She would happily take on the role on a purely voluntary basis. As she saw it, by taking certain trivial matters out of his hands, she would be instrumental in encouraging him to write more plays. And that was more than enough reward for Annie.

Yeats was a leading figure in the Irish National Theatre Society, and on October 5th 1903, when his play *The King's Threshold* was staged in Dublin, Annie was in close support. She even made the costumes.

And so impressed was she with the high artistic standard of the Irish National Theatre Society, which at that time had no permanent home, that she felt she had to do something constructive and positive to foster this spirit – to provide them with a permanent theatre.

So, at a cost of some £13,000, she took over and renovated a derelict hall in Dublin and in December 1904, the Abbey Theatre was born.

Not only was the Irish National Theatre granted free use of it, but they were paid an annual subsidy of £600, which was to continue for many years. The freehold was eventually transferred to the trustees for £1,000.

In addition to the annual subsidy for the theatre, without which it couldn't have survived, Annie's money also provided the various technical resources required. It facilitated the development of a professional and talented repertory company which enabled them to produce plays which commercial companies would have been unable to consider staging, and to undertake tours which spread the Abbey name outside Ireland.

The Abbey Theatre went on to forge an international reputation. Theatre business was, however, hampered by internal disputes, one of the more serious being over the level of control Annie Horniman wished to exercise.

Matters eventually came to a head, Annie withdrew her subsidy and this led to a bitter legal dispute over sums of money owed. And her close friendship with Yeats was never subsequently renewed.

When her father died in 1906, and left a further sizable legacy to Annie, she could see her way to realising her greatest ambition. To create a dramatic, artistic venture based on repertory principles, that, unlike the Abbey Theatre, would be run on commercial lines.

But the big question was where?

Annie decided to look to the success of the Irish National Theatre for inspiration. While the Irish players had been on tour, one city stood out from the rest when it came to support and enthusiasm for their work. A city that had proved repeatedly that it had a taste for the arts and an avid appetite for innovation. The taste for culture was underlined by the popular support for the acclaimed orchestra of Charles Halle.

It was, of course, Manchester.

But Manchester already had a number of theatres which were served quite well by touring productions, often featuring the big names of the day.

And it was important that Annie Horniman's experiment should succeed not only culturally, but also financially. So where did her ideas fit into the existing scheme of things?

And how would they differ sufficiently from what was already on offer to attract enough theatregoers to ensure its financial success?

What Annie planned to give to the people of Manchester was a repertory theatre, with a regular change of programme performed by a permanent company of actors. There would be no long-running plays. No stars. What the theatre-going public would see would be a vast number of fine plays by a wide variety of authors, efficiently produced and at prices that would be popular to all.

It was also her intention that many British authors who had hitherto tried in vain to have their work performed in public would be adequately represented.

The aims were clear, the enthusiasm unquestionable – and she had the money to launch such a venture. What more could Annie need? In a word, a theatre.

At this point in time it wasn't possible to find one vacant week in any of the existing Manchester venues. They were all solidly booked for the season with touring productions.

But Annie was a determined lady, and by July 1907, she was able to announce that her company would commence work in the autumn with a series of productions at the Midland Hotel in Manchester city centre.

The Midland Hotel housed a theatre because the Gentleman's Concert Hall had previously stood on the site. When the hotel was built, the theatre facilities that had been provided by the Gentleman's Concert Hall were built into it.

The theatre at the Midland Hotel was booked initially for four weeks. And the new Manchester Playgoers Theatre opened its first season in September with plays by Shaw, French playwright Edmond Rostand, Irish playwright Charles McEvoy and David Ballard. So successful was the season that it was extended for a further week.

The big question now was: 'Where do we go from here?'

As if in answer to Miss Horniman's prayers, a solution presented itself sooner than she could ever have hoped for.

Before the Midland Hotel season was over, she was able to break the news that she had bought the Gaiety Theatre just a stone's throw away.

The company was not to take possession of the Gaiety until March the following year, so when the final curtain came down on the short Midland Hotel season, the company packed up and took their productions on tour to many major cities in the United Kingdom, as well as Dublin.

This was to become the pattern of operation for many years to come – a season in Manchester followed by a tour which would take all the plays they had presented so successfully in repertory in the city to the rest of the country, and before long, across the Atlantic, too.

But it would take many months to make all the changes to the theatre that Annie wanted, and it would not be possible to open properly before the Autumn. So they arranged a short season of plays earlier in the year, so that the goodwill and support they had created at the Midland Hotel would not be lost, and it would also allow them to establish themselves in their new home. After that, the company would go on tour.

When the refurbished Gaiety opened on September 9th 1908 it was indeed a magnificent theatre. Annie's repertoire of plays was wide and varied – Greek tragedies, classics, translations of foreign plays as well as contemporary plays by new playwrights, many from the north of England who saw their work performed publicly for the first time, Harold Brighouse's *Hobson's Choice*, and Stanley Haughton's *Hindle Wakes* among them.

Annie's actors were chosen because they could act. There were no stars as she intended, although inevitably actors of stature did emerge to secure for themselves a place in theatrical history.

The repertory theatre experiment soon spread to other provincial cities, and the Gaiety Theatre and Manchester was acclaimed as the foundation stone of the repertory movement.

Annie Horniman became a well-known figure in Manchester, developing her skills as a public speaker, addressing various groups and societies. She was always ready to offer her opinion on many subjects, particularly on issues connected with the theatre and drama, as well as on the women's suffrage movement, of which she was still a passionate supporter.

In 1910, her contribution to the cultural life of Manchester was honoured by Manchester University when she was awarded an Honorary MA degree.

She did make a brief appearance herself on stage in a non-speaking part, when she played herself in *Nothing Like Leather*, Alan Monkhouse's satire on the Gaiety and those associated with it. After receiving an ovation, she remembered the occasion as one of the greatest moments of her life.

But although there was no doubt about the Gaiety's critical success, as the war years loomed, there were growing financial problems as audiences began to drop.

Although Annie took the decline in the Gaiety's fortunes as a fresh challenge, and renewed her efforts to keep her company going, she and her team were unable to overcome the long-term effects of wartime.

By 1917, Annie Horniman was left with no option but to bow to the inevitable. Her company was disbanded. Once again, the Gaiety became a theatre where touring productions could find temporary lodgings.

Annie, however, was convinced that this was only a temporary setback, and that after the war it would only be a matter of time before the Gaiety Theatre and Miss Horniman's players were once again in the forefront of the Manchester entertainment scene.

But when peace returned, it soon became obvious that this was not to be. Too few people were prepared to provide financial support. The high cost of mounting touring productions, a newly-introduced entertainment tax together with the popularity of the movies, left her with no alternative but to sell her beloved theatre.

But before the curtain fell on live entertainment at the Gaiety, for the last time, the new owners decided to present one last season of repertory plays. Ironically, they played to full houses. But it made no difference to the ultimate fate of the theatre. The final curtain came down at the end of the season in 1921, before the Gaiety was sold to a cinema chain.

Annie Horniman had seen her dream become reality, only for it to fade again in the very city where it had all been made possible – Manchester. But she established in the city a reputation for critical acclaim that lives on to this very day.

While she remained an avid theatregoer for the rest of her life, after the Gaiety was sold she never became actively involved again.

After she left the Gaiety, she indulged her other great passion – travelling throughout Europe. And she was a frequent visitor to Germany, the country she had come to adore so much and the homeland of the governess who had unwittingly started a revolution in the English theatre when she took a 13-year-old girl and her brother on a clandestine trip to see *The Merchant of Venice.*

Annie Horniman could be obstinate, outspoken and stubborn, often refusing to compromise or accept half measures. But she showed great loyalty and endless generosity both in her personal and her professional life.

She was always ready to offer financial help to her friends, always ready to fund worthwhile theatrical ventures. She worked tirelessly to achieve her ideals, along the way launching the careers of many actors and authors who went on to become leading figures in the world of theatre.

Acknowledged as one of the most powerful influences in the shaping of British theatre in the 20th Century, she received national recognition for her work in 1933 when she was created a Companion of Honour.

Annie Horniman died in her sleep on August 6th, 1937. She was 76.

5

FROM REP TO THE ROVERS

THE MAJORITY OF actors I had the pleasure of working with who came from a rep theatre background were undoubtedly jacks of all trades, not only as actors but in all fields of stagecraft.

They may have come into the profession as a child actor, through drama school or from amateur dramatics. They all had one thing in common – they were all well capable of doing just about any task dropped on them.

They had to be. They had probably joined their first company as assistant stage manager/actor. They would hope that sooner rather than later they would get their first lines on the professional stage. And as ASM, they would be hoping that they would be working with an experienced stage manager who knew the job inside out and could pass on all the tricks of the trade, of which there were more than you would find in a magician's trunk.

The reality was that there was no way the smaller companies would have stretched to such luxury as a stage manager <u>and</u> an assistant. The young newcomer was definitely thrown in at the deep end.

They just had to pick it up as they went along, but not without some advice. Most of the actors in the company had come along the same path, and there would be one or two at least who would be happy to offer words of encouragement and support. It was in their interests after all, because if the ASM wasn't doing their job, it would be down to the cast to pick up the pieces.

As stage manager, they would be responsible for just about any task imaginable to ensure the smooth day-to-day running of the company – or they would at least be expected to take a reasonable stab at it.

They would find themselves responsible for the sound effects, which could be many and diverse – telephone cues. approaching footsteps, departing footsteps, doors opening, doors closing, cars arriving, cars departing, gunshots, shop bells, bicycle bells, church bells, ice cream bells and so the list went on. And, as and when needed, music.

In fact anything the play called for – and for which they would get no credit. The audience took sound effects for granted – until something went wrong.

Music could be fairly straightforward, depending on the production, of course. If the show was a musical, that was a different story and called for a lot of skilful timing. But for the ordinary run-of-the-mill play put on by the average weekly rep company, the plot was simple.

Just before the front of house curtain went up, play the opening bars. Just before the end of the scene, play it again and carry it right through to when the curtain came down.

It was most important to bring the music up to full volume as the curtain came down for the interval. That way you would get maximum applause.

And curtain cues could be any one of three speeds depending on the mood of the play, slow, medium or fast, though much depended on the age of the equipment.

One seasoned stage manager who had absolutely relished sound effects told me that after a while it all became less of a mystery. But his job would have been made a lot easier if the company had boasted a record library of more than just two discs – *Skaters Waltz* and *Dance Macabre*!

The stage manager – or rather assistant stage manager, who

was expected to do the same job, but for less money – would also more than likely be involved with the lighting director, should the company be fortunate enough to have one, in setting the lighting plot for the play.

A set was not lit accidentally. All the technical jargon had to be learned, and for the effects to be convincing, a lot of thought and planning was needed.

They could be looking for a myriad of effects, from the opening to the final curtain, creating the right lighting for a seemingly endless stream of situations and moods – morning, afternoon, evening.

Was a scene set in daylight, darkness or somewhere in between? Did the action call for sunshine, moonlight or a variety of other effects? What was the mood of the play? What was the mood of each scene?

It was all aimed at adding authenticity and maximising dramatic effect throughout the production, adding a very important dimension for audience and actors alike.

One of the most important attributes needed by the ASM was diplomacy. The ability to get on with all the other members of the company at all times, otherwise their indiscretion may come back to haunt them. They would be responsible for the erection of the set – and if they had rubbed folk up the wrong way, they may well find themselves doing the job single-handed, which could be a nightmare when it came to handling the larger flats on a windy day with the dock door wide open!

They would even paint it when it needed freshening up – the set, that is, not the dock door, though no doubt some would have been cajoled into doing that as well on occasion.

They would be responsible for acquiring and setting the practical props, for setting the stage, making sure that furniture and fittings were properly placed, hanging drapes at the windows, sweeping the stage, laying carpets, polishing the furniture – the list of jobs must have seemed endless to the new recruit. Then just when they felt that they had thought of everything, along came another set of responsibilities.

Are the windows practical? Do they need to be opened and closed? If so, do they open inwards or outwards? And most important, doors. Which way were they supposed to open – and they did have to open when required, every time. This may seem to be a fairly straightforward matter, but door frames in a stage set are not built into bricks and mortar. A door can be functioning perfectly one night, and the next night it would have a mind of its own.

And the rewards for all this forethought and hard work? Not a lot. Comments when the actors saw the set for the first time could be less than encouraging.

'That door opens the wrong way.'

'How am I going to be able to see him from here?'

'Why isn't there a door here? That's the way I've rehearsed it all week.'

'Is this supposed to be a desk? It looks more like a wash stand!'

But they knew that their reward would come eventually when they got what they joined the company for in the first place – their first line in a production!

One of the first things that the assistant stage manager learned when entering the profession was that if it could go wrong, it probably would. And whatever it was, from a sticking cupboard to a missed cue or misplaced prop, the finger would probably point unwaveringly at the beleaguered ASM!

Yet somehow, they survived. Because everyone in the company had been through the same experience at some time or other and when it came to closing ranks to cope with adversity, there was no doubting their loyalty to each other.

There was a very special feel about a small-town rep company. They were all in it together. They may squabble among themselves from time to time, but when it came to their public persona, they would stick together to the bitter end. The theatre became home to the actors who worked there, the members of the company were family.

This sense of camaraderie would more often than not continue throughout their careers in the entertainment business. I came across it in television. When we started work on a new series, coming together as a company for the first time, generally everyone would quickly get to know each other, share each other's thoughts and feelings, offer support where needed as we all strove to make the best of whatever show we were working on.

As we got to know each other better, we would go out for meals, talk about our families and if we were working away, frequently stay in each other's homes.

Then at the end of the run, we would say our goodbyes and all go our separate ways.

There may be the odd Christmas card, and general invitation 'If you are ever down my way, look me up.' But rarely did it happen.

But the next time we met up with someone we had worked with before, old friendships and relationships were quickly re-kindled in the genuine warmth of rediscovery.

It was almost as if we had never parted.

There were exceptions, of course. You occasionally came across actors who just didn't want to get involved with the others. They would come into studio, do the job and go with hardly a word to anyone. That was just their way.

But they were definitely in the minority. I know of friendships that were forged in some theatre or TV production 40 years ago that still endure to this day.

6

BUDGET? WHAT BUDGET? THIS IS REP

A GREAT FRIEND of mine was Peter Adamson, who, after a long career in weekly rep, found fame as Len Fairclough in *Coronation Street*.

When we met up on the set of *Corrie*, it wasn't the first time our paths had crossed. We had known each other in a previous life that had centred on the Sale Palace Theatre repertory company in Cheshire. It was an excellent illustration of the camaraderie I have mentioned. We spent many an hour reminiscing about those days when the local weekly rep company was almost as much a part of folk's lives as *Coronation Street* was to become.

Peter's route into the profession was fairly typical of many other young people with their eyes set on an acting career.

After becoming interested in drama in his youth through radio and going to professional plays in Liverpool where he lived, he became involved in amateur dramatics before going to the London Academy of Music and Dramatic Art. His family were unable to contribute, so while he was there he had to virtually live hand to mouth to afford the fees and be able to support himself.

After he left LAMDA, he started to look for his first professional work, and when he saw an advertisement for an assistant stage manager/actor with the Frank H Fortescue Players at Bury, he was to take the first steps in what was to be a long and distinguished career in theatre and television.

And he didn't have to wait long for his first lines on the professional stage.

His first speaking part with the Frank H Fortesque Players was in a crime thriller. He was handed four pieces of grubby brown paper on which were his lines. Rehearsals started the following day in the upstairs room at the pub across the road from the theatre.

He dutifully learned his lines, then turned his attention to the stage management. He made sure that everything was in the right place, all the doors and windows opened the way they should do. Finally, most important, he made sure that he had all his own personal props – hat, cigarette case, two cigarettes a notebook and a belted raincoat.

The raincoat was on a coat stand stage left, the side on which most of the entrances and exits were to be made. During the dress rehearsal, almost inevitably every time anyone entered or left the set, the coat was knocked to the floor. For some artistic reason that no one could explain, it wasn't acceptable for the coat stand to be repositioned, so before the play opened on the first night, some kind soul fastened the belt round the stand to make sure the coat stayed put.

But whoever did it didn't tell Peter.

The big moment arrived – his first performance as a professional actor.

He delivered his brief lines, grabbed his coat as he made his exit – and dragged the raincoat, the stand and half the set behind him!

His professional debut was certainly one that he would never forget.

It wasn't unusual for the ASM to get thrown in at the deep end without any consideration being given as to whether it was his first job or not.

Another of the actors from my theatre club started life in

the professional theatre when he answered an advertisement for an assistant stage manager, heard nothing for a fortnight, had more or less written it off when he got a telegram telling him to get to a theatre in Lancashire immediately.

That was on Thursday. When he got there, there was no time for niceties or induction ceremonies. They were opening with a new play on the following Monday, he was handed a list of props and told to get on with it.

Trying to sound constructive, he tentatively inquired about the budget, to which he received the emphatic reply 'Budget? What budget? This is weekly rep.'

If he was going to keep his job, he could forget all thought of anything like that.

To the young ASM going into his first job, being a living part of the professional theatre for which he had yearned for so long, was at the same time both terrifying and exciting.

But on the plus side, from the very outset he would be treated just the same as everyone else, as a fully-fledged member of the profession.

One thing that every rep company had in common was a wide repertoire of plays.

And the actors may sometimes find themselves trying to get their heads around three plays at the same time.

As well as the one they were performing that week, they would be reading and rehearsing the play for the following week. And they may also put on an additional performance of something that everyone was expected to know, should conditions warrant it. This was particularly true of seaside companies if the weather was poor.

The company may well find themselves opening the week on a Monday with a murder mystery. At quarter past ten on Tuesday morning, they would prepare to read through and block the following week's play, which could be a complete contrast – change of character, change of atmosphere and change of mood. From dark drama to comedy, from mystery and suspense to farce.

The company would probably have been given their copies of the play for the following week after the Monday night's performance and told which part they would be playing.

After the initial read-through on the Tuesday morning, the afternoon would be spent studying acts one and two of that play, while in the evening, they would be performing the murder mystery again.

On the Wednesday morning, they would run through the first two acts of the following week's play. Barring any unforeseen crises, Wednesday afternoon would probably be free time. Thursday morning, after another run through, was usually free to allow time for study, while Thursday afternoon would be set aside for the collection of props.

And Friday was usually dress rehearsal, and the day of the week that everyone looked forward to – the day the ghost walked. Pay day.

And it was usually on a Friday that there would sometimes be the added attraction of an extra late-night performance, often a melodrama.

The money in rep was not good, and after paying for digs the actors had to be careful how they spent what little was left. It wasn't uncommon for a young actor to spend half his weekly pay packet on accommodation.

The rest didn't go far. As well as being responsible for providing their own personal props for each play, the actors were also expected to dress well both off and on stage.

For the men, that usually meant having a lounge suit, dinner suit, sports outfit, blazer, flannels, and a range of sports gear ranging from jodhpurs to running kit. For the girls, a selection of dress for winter or summer, day wear, evening wear, formal and informal, as well as a range of sports wear.

And who paid for all the wardrobe they needed? They did. On the occasions the play called for period costume, it would usually mean a trip to the nearest theatrical costume hire shop or the local amateur dramatic society for help.

Local markets and charity shops were the most popular source of clothing, and there must have been many a well-heeled fashion-conscious woman who would have been amazed to know that her latest donation to Oxfam would within days be playing a starring role in the current local rep company offering.

My first contact with the rep scene, and as it was to turn out, with one of the biggest stars of *Coronation Street*, was through our local repertory company in Cheshire.

Peter Adamson, who was to go on to become one of the strongest characters in the Street as builder Len Fairclough, was at the time a stalwart of the company and I a mere schoolboy.

Neither of us could have had an inkling that we would one day meet up again and work as colleagues on the greatest drama serial in the history of television.

At the time of our first meeting, I and my pals from school used to go to a local coffee shop which was also used by the actors from the theatre. We used to do our collective homework by a sort of committee process, while the boys and girls from the theatre were relaxing or going through their lines.

They would pool their limited resources to buy a single pot of tea, ask for as many cups as they needed and an endless supply of hot water.

We weren't a part of the theatre or the company, but through our regular meetings over a pot of tea in The Coffee

Pot and the common ground that bound us – poverty – we got to know each other quite well. We were accepted. We became one of them.

And although they had precious little in the way of material goods, whatever they did have, like the occasional packet of biscuits,, they were happy to share, even occasionally paying for our tea when we were finding times particularly tough.

I did manage to pay them back in my own small way. I was into photography at the time, and I eventually found myself doing front of house pictures for the theatre – an honorary position, I might add.

But despite the difficulties, the long hours, the lack of money I never came across one actor who had been through the hardships of the rep system at that time who would have swapped the experience for anything.

Peter was not the only member of that company who I was to meet again through my work in television. For the most part they were just fleeting moments in the corridors of a studio. But, as soon as we set eyes on each other, we were the best of mates again. You would have thought it was only yesterday that we last saw each other.

But on these occasions, there was a slight difference in our relationship.

It was usually me who paid for the tea!

7

NOW WHERE HAVE I SEEN HIM BEFORE?

MOST OF THE members of the cast of *Coronation Street* had learned their craft in the rep theatres.

And many companies in the greater Manchester area, notably Oldham Rep and its associated Theatre Workshop, Bolton Octagon, Manchester Library Theatre, have been a constant source of talent for TV casting directors.

During my years on the show, the backgrounds of many of our cast members before they decided on an acting career were as diverse as the roles they played.

The girls may have been waitresses, worked in bars or as models. They may have had previous experience as child actors, maybe appeared in musicals. Some had even appeared in the West End, while at least one had started out on a career as a ballet dancer. Language student, librarian, drama teacher, secretary, even a TV presenter – the variety was endless.

The men, too, came from equally unlikely backgrounds – window cleaner, shop assistant, textile worker, draughtsman, engineer, stand-up comic.

They may have worked in radio, come straight from drama school, theatre workshop or appeared in amateur dramatics before joining their first professional companies. The one thing they had in common was that they wanted to act and would take any opportunity to work at it.

Whichever route they took into the acting profession, few could have dreamed when they took their first tentative steps in their chosen profession that one day they would achieve worldwide recognition playing to audiences of millions as the result of appearing in a television drama serial set in the most famous street in the world.

During the early 1950s, theatre clubs started to emerge. Regular theatregoers became 'members' of their local rep theatre, and had the same seats week in, week out, usually at a discounted rate. For the theatre company, it provided a guaranteed audience, or, more importantly if there was a week when not everyone turned up because of the weather, some other commitment or just because they didn't fancy that week's offering, a guaranteed income at the box office.

For some of the smaller companies, audiences could be very much an unknown quantity. Nevertheless, the actors were professionals who would put on a performance for whoever turned up. If there were only a dozen in the audience, the play still went on.

The audiences loved this sense of belonging. They were a part of their local theatre 'family'. They belonged to the actors, and the actors belonged to them.

If they saw the actors out and about, they would chat to them, buy them a drink. They used to turn up, week in, week out, eager to see which parts the actors were playing that week. Sometimes, the company would slip in a bit of business that was obviously not in the play to make that night's theatregoers feel special.

And such was the fondness the audience had for the performers, that they readily forgave any mistakes the actors made.

They were never too critical. For one thing, in their experience for the most part they didn't have anything to compare the performances with, except star-studded Hollywood productions and there was never any pretence to emulate them.

I recall one play that called for a light aircraft to 'crash' on stage. This wasn't a Cameron McIntosh production in a West End theatre for four years, where every known piece of computer-controlled, mechanical and electronic wizardry could be built into the extravagant set. This was our weekly rep. Opened on the Monday, closed on the Saturday, following an Agatha Christie murder mystery the week before and giving way to a farce the following week. Money was scarce. Sets and props had to be built with a mixture of scrap materials and ingenuity.

So a contraption was built in sections that could be assembled quickly to form some semblance of a stricken aircraft between the end of the short first act and the opening of the second act, which would herald the start of the action in earnest. And it was remarkably convincing, considering the restraints.

As the curtain came down on the first act, the stage manager would assemble the sections to create the wreckage, start up the sound effects, open the tabs and the second act would get underway. It wasn't the whole 'aircraft' – just enough of it to convince the audience that somewhere off stage left was the rest of the mangled remains.

Unfortunately, it didn't go according to plan every night. The only one who knew how to assemble the wreckage in the right order and in reasonable time was the ageing stage manager, who had never progressed any further up the career ladder, nor did he ever have any wish to do so. And there was no way he was going to let anyone else in on the secret.

There was just one slight problem. He was rather fond of an after dinner drink. And one before dinner, one before and after lunch and no doubt one before and after breakfast as well.

The result was that the wreckage failed to appear for two performances because the stage manager wasn't there to assemble it! They just had to make do with one small section of 'fuselage'.

But nobody got steamed up about it.

The actors got on with the action, the audience on those nights happily accepted that somewhere just off stage were the remains of the aircraft that was central to the action, and there was no way the non-appearance of the contraption detracted one jot from their enjoyment of the occasion. In fact, the company drew many a plaudit for making the play so convincing without the central prop!

Ingenuity and improvisation was the name of the game in weekly rep – it had to be, because of the financial constraints they operated under.

But far from being fazed by the endless challenges that presented themselves, the young, eager ASM saw each one as a new test of his or her ingenuity, one more way to prove their creativity and inventiveness.

Whenever a play was being performed that was lacking in action, every trick was used to brighten it up with special effects from the available resources. Sound effects were particularly useful – lightning, thunder crashes, creaking doors, storm effects.

That was when the sound equipment was working.

There was one production that called for the Police Inspector to make an entrance in the last scene to arrest the villain. It was a tense, dramatic climax to a heavy drama. The family were all assembled in the living room, awaiting the final showdown. The action called for voices on stage to be raised, then silenced in anticipation as the sound effects heralded the arrival of visitors.

The off-stage sound effects should have been car arriving, engine being switched off, car doors being opened, car doors being slammed as the players on stage maintained a total

silence, exchanging anxious glances as they waited expectantly for the inevitable knock at the door.

But on the Friday night, the ancient equipment that played
the recordings finally gave up the ghost. Sound effects were
off the menu.

The actor on stage delivered his cue line. Nothing.

He spoke it again, this time with more purpose. Still
nothing.

After a further brief pause, accompanied by muffled voices
off stage, the silence was broken by a fierce hammering on
the door, which was opened by a member of the family to
let in the Inspector and his Sergeant. Bristling with fury, the
Inspector delivered his opening line:

'My name is Inspector Sharp. This is Sergeant May.'

Then after a purposeful pause –

'And we've come all the way from the village on our bikes!'

One of my favourite stories came out of a play set in the
Civil War. I can't vouch for its authenticity, as I have heard it
from more than one source, but it is worth re-telling anyway.
It sums up improvisation perfectly.

A servant was to murder an Army officer by stabbing him.

At the crucial point in the play as the pair confronted each
other, the servant muttered sotto voce to his superior:

'I forgot the dagger'.

The officer was thrown for a minute.

'What?'

'I forgot the dagger,' came the whispered reply.

'Kick me,' said his intended victim, after barely a moment's
thought.

'Kick me. In the shin.'

The baffled servant did as he was told.

'Ahh,' screamed the officer as he clutched at his leg.

'What treachery. A poison boot.'

And he promptly collapsed onto the stage!

To relieve their own monotony, or provide a special welcome to a new, young member of the company, the actors would now and again come up with something unexpected. It had to be a young actor – all the older ones were wise to every trick ever pulled on stage.

One night, a member of the cast put a whoopee cushion under the real cushion on a chair.

After the first victim sat down to an unscheduled sound effect, much to her embarrassment and the obvious delight of the audience, the rest of the cast would run a competition among themselves to find the most inventive reason for not sitting down on that chair for the rest of the play.

The audience loved it.

Another old rep actor recalled one night when his company were performing a melodrama set in Cornwall about three wayward brothers, one of whom had made a local girl pregnant.

At one point in the play, the boy arrived at the girl's home to confront her and her mother. The girl, having had a near-hysterical scene with her mother and not wanting to even set eyes on the boy, had fled in tears to hide in a cupboard under the stairs.

As the mother was lashing the hapless young man with the thick edge of her tongue, asking how he could ever have thought of doing such a thing to such a poor innocent child, the sobs from the cupboard became louder and louder.

Heavy with guilt, the lad went to the cupboard to try to console the distraught young lass. The atmosphere was heavy with tension as he prepared himself to deliver his next line in solemn tones:

'It was a terrible thing that I did to you, lass. Can you ever forgive me?'

He sheepishly opened the cupboard door and there inside, unseen by the audience, the actress was standing with her back towards him, knickers round her knees with a face painted on her backside and a clay pipe protruding from – well I think you get the picture!

On another occasion, an elderly actor who that particular week didn't have a lot to do and was well known for enjoying a spot of liquid refreshment every time he left the stage, stopped the action by walking to the front of the stage and solemnly asking the audience:

'Is there a doctor in the house?'

When a volunteer eventually stood up, much to the relief of the shocked audience, the old actor came out with:

'And what do you think of it so far, doctor?'

He was playing a murder victim in one play, in which he 'died' at the end of the first act. He expired having supped from the poison chalice, which the actor was quite happy about. He was happy to sup from anything. It was another opportunity for a swift nip of his favourite tipple, of which he had already had more than was good for him.

His moment came, he clutched at his throat, slumped onto the stage in a very convincing performance – until the descending curtain jammed.

He lay there prostrate as the curtain was at first slowly lowered until it stuck about two thirds the way down. Eventually, after much jerking and tugging, accompanied by a lot of off-stage expletives, the curtain was released and dropped with a crash inches from the actor's head.

At which point, the 'corpse' sat bolt upright and bellowed 'You bastard. You could have f***ing well killed me!'

8

SIX BIKES? YOU MUST BE JOKING

WITH A FAIRLY tight budget, any props that were needed that hadn't been acquired by the company over the years and were readily to hand had to be begged or borrowed from local suppliers.

In return, the obliging tradesmen would get a mention in the programme, free tickets, or both. It cost the company nothing. It had to. Props budgets were practically non-existent.

But despite what they considered to be their unbridled generosity to their benefactors, the company didn't always get exactly what they wanted.

In a production of a play set in the Swiss Alps, featuring three couples on holiday, one scene called for all six members of the cast to arrive on bicycles.

Unfortunately, the ASM couldn't persuade the local bike shop to part with six bicycles. They didn't even come up with two. The best they could offer was two sets of handlebars.

So the ASM built a ground row – a piece of scenery that stood at about waist height – that ran more or less the width of the stage. This would hide the lower part of the actors' bodies from the audience.

The first two crossed the stage, legs unseen by the audience, gripping the handlebars, backs arched as they 'pedalled' from one side to the other. They passed the handlebars to the ASM, who was just off stage, and over a couple of lines of chat between the first two actors, he would race round the back to hand them to the next couple, who would then cross the stage in similar fashion to the first couple, before the process was repeated again until all six had 'cycled' across the stage.

The three couples then strode into the centre of the set laughing and joking and continued with the action!

I don't think they fooled a single member of the audience for one minute, but as I have mentioned, the playgoers were very understanding and ever appreciative of the efforts by the company to make do and mend in the interests of putting on a convincing performance.

For the company's part, they were ever trying to brighten up performances at every opportunity with any special effect they could come up with.

But not all of them had the desired effect.

The biggest buzz in the theatre for many actors comes as they hear the audience arriving as curtain up approaches. There is nothing like the build up of chatter and anticipation as the auditorium fills to get the adrenalin flowing.

The most eerie time is frequently after rehearsal, when everyone has left the theatre.

But this is also a time when an enterprising stage manager can try out additional effects that will enhance the production. I should perhaps say ASM, because they were generally young, enthusiastic and keen to make their mark in the profession, willing to try anything to come up with something special that would add to the performance. The seasoned stage manager would be much more likely to leave well alone, knowing full well through years of experience that if something can go wrong it will, without any additional help from him.

So innovation usually came from the ASM as he or she strove to make a name for themselves, unfortunately not always with 100 per cent success.

The company was presenting *Dracula*, which, to the inventive mind of the young ASM, presented many opportunities for special effects to heighten the dramatic impact on the audience.

He had worked out a system of pulleys on the drapes at the French windows, so that every time Dracula appeared they would open and close seemingly by themselves. He worked out how they could do the stake through the heart business and make it spurt blood. But he felt that the most powerful effect in instilling terror in the audience would be that of a vampire bat flying out over the auditorium in near-total darkness as the play opened, if it could be achieved.

And to the eager young ASM nothing is impossible.

He waited for rehearsals to finish, and when he had the theatre to himself, he set to work.

He took a length of quarter inch elastic and attached it to heavy-duty screw eyes either side of the stage just behind the line of the front tabs.

He got hold of an umbrella, took out the spokes and made the 'bat'.

What remained of the umbrella handle was attached to the elastic, which he pulled back like a catapult and let go. The 'bat' flapped out over the auditorium and came back again – a very realistic effect.

He tried it again and again and it worked perfectly. All set for opening night.

As the play opened on the first night, the lights went down, the music faded, the tabs were drawn open and with the theatre in almost total darkness, the ASM pulled back the elastic, released his 'bat' – and the entire contraption flapped out in the direction of the audience. Only this time, it didn't come back!

He had certainly achieved what he had set out to do. He had produced an element of surprise and fear. What he hadn't intended was for one unfortunate theatregoer to have had the fright of his life as he was subjected to an unprovoked and totally unexpected attack by a rampant umbrella in full flight!

After the show, the ASM waited in trepidation for the victim to come round to vent his anger, or worse, to threaten to sue the company for inflicting untold injuries. But no one appeared. He couldn't believe his luck. The next day, the cleaner told the ASM that someone had left an umbrella behind the previous night. She had found it near the back of the theatre, and had put it in the bin. Why on earth anyone would carry round an umbrella that was totally useless beat her!

And there was no way the ASM was going to take the slightest risk with his special effects after that.

For the average company, eight to ten actors was just about normal – leading man, leading lady, leading character man, leading character lady and so on.

And on occasion, some companies had to manage with fewer than that.

So there were times when an actor may find himself playing more than one part, and many an occasion when a large dose of ingenuity was called for.

As in one murder mystery, which called for eleven characters – but the company only had eight.

So one actor doubled up in two parts, and two characters were cut out altogether.

Lines suddenly appeared like:

'Have you seen the professor?'

'He never leaves his room, you know.'

'I haven't seen the doctor's wife this morning.'

'She's gone down to the village for a paper.'

But at no time was improvisation and ingenuity needed more than when a local rep company decided to stage a pantomime.

With their limited resources, not many small companies even attempted pantomime, particularly if they were in big towns. While the seasonal treat was no problem for the larger theatres with their bigger budgets and facility for lavish productions, if you were running a small town rep with a company of eight permanent players, there was no way you were going to compete with that lot.

But this didn't stop one or two of them putting on a pantomime all the same. Despite the constraints of cast and budget, they would want to give their loyal, regular audience something different, so for one week – two at the most – they would put on an annual seasonal treat.

It was little wonder, then, that audiences were treated to shows like *Snow White and the Four Dwarfs!*

But my personal favourite has to be the staging of *Ali Baba and the Forty Thieves*, which led to numerous scenes where Ali Baba called off stage:

'You two come with me. The rest of you . . . stop there!'

9

END OF AN ERA

BY THE MID 1950s, much of small town rep was in decline. Audiences were dwindling and many theatres were in their death throes. The total wage bill may have been little more than £100 per week, but it still spelt financial disaster.

Television had arrived.

The Coronation in 1953 had shown the nation and the world what could be achieved.

Theatre-going had largely been a habit with many folk, particularly those who belonged to the weekly rep theatre clubs.

And with the growing influence of television, more and more people were staying at home and the theatre-going habit was broken. Initially, this falling off of audiences was not seen as a major threat. There had been occasional hiccups in the past, but they had always bounced back again, and generally they had been playing to good houses for years.

But this time was different. The traditional rep audiences had a wider choice of entertainment than they had ever had before without ever having to leave the comfort of their front rooms.

When the company took a week off while the theatre was being given its annual face lift, or the amateur operatic society moved in to present its yearly offering, the regular audience usually came flooding back when the weekly rep programme resumed. Now it was taking three or four weeks to build up again, if they were lucky.

Once independent television had taken a hold, some companies never got the audiences back at all.

For many theatres, the end was in sight. Reminiscing with Peter Adamson about his days in rep, he recalled that as audiences dwindled and jobs became more and more scarce, he delivered closure speeches from the stages of 13 different theatres.

My local rep company was no exception. The total wage bill was £114 a week, but it was a financial disaster.

Not all the rep companies which had reached their peak of popularity during the years following the second world war closed down, of course. Many carried on, thrived and are still strongly supported today, mainly in bigger towns, cities and seaside resorts. And the movement has been further strengthend with many more theatre groups taking advantage of the many new facilities that have been built since the war, not only on conventional lines. And many of those companies and their associated youth theatres are providing writers, directors, actors, designers and technicians with the opportunity to produce innovative and experimental drama that is at the cutting age of modern theatre.

There is still many an actor making a living doing a summer season in seaside rep, then moving to a bigger inland town for the winter season or pantomime.

And there are still actor-managers working in these theatres, who came up through the acknowledged route of assistant stage manager, stage manager, walk-on, full time actor, before producing and eventually managing their own company.

It wasn't just the advent of television that sealed the fate of many of the smaller rep companies running on a shoestring. Many theatres had been built in the early 1920s or earlier, and were desperately in need of renovation and refurbishment, calling for injections of cash that was just not available.

As television began to make its presence felt, the whole acting business was changing. Many young people coming into the profession had their eyes firmly fixed on the lucrative world of television drama rather than getting on with the job of being a jobbing actor in a rep company. They had their sights set on films and television from the outset.

I heard of a number of actors at that time who had turned down a small town theatre season somewhere because to take it may mean them missing out on a television job. It was not uncommon for many to loftily announce that they were going to concentrate on television. Nor was it surprising to the old pros that many of them were never seen or heard of again. The actors who did eventually make it into television were generally those who carried on working in their chosen profession in whatever role came up, wherever the venue.

For some of the old hands, appearing in front of the cameras was not a new experience, particularly in my part of the world.

Round about the same time that Annie Horniman was establishing her Gaiety Theatre in Manchester, market trader James Blakeley was taking his first steps in the entertainment business in London when he opened a cinema.

It was probably nothing spectacular, not much more than rows of benches, a projector and a sheet for a screen. But it gave him a start, he drew the audiences and he could see there was money to be made from films.

Shortly afterwards, he set up a film rental company with his two sons, James Jnr and John E Blakeley.

It turned out to be a great success, with John becoming increasingly influential in the family business as he effectively demonstrated that he had the knack of knowing exactly what the public wanted to see, and providing it for them.

The next stage was almost inevitable. In 1927, John spearheaded the family's venture into the film-making business when he set out to shoot his first silent films, which also turned out to be a great success and led him on to the next stage of his spectacular career – making a full length feature film.

The film was *Two Little Drummer Boys* starring Wee Georgie Wood which was also a massive hit, quickly recouping its costs.

Wee Georgie Wood was a comic of tiny stature, only 4 ft 9 ins tall. and it was probably he who was the first adult to play a boy character. Others followed, of course, who went on to become big names in theatre, radio and television, perhaps most notably Stan Little, Jimmy Clitheroe and latterly Jeanette Tough of The Krankies.

With the advent of sound, further opportunities presented themselves, and John set about achieving his ambition of making the most of the vast array of talent that was emerging, particularly from the north of England.

The films at that time were being shot in London, but there was no doubt that the northern audiences were the most appreciative of his output. And John was in no doubt as to where the future of his film-making lay. As his objective loomed increasingly large, the name of the company was changed to the Mancunian Film Corporation Ltd as he set out to fulfil his dream. To one day be making northern films with northern talent for northern folk in a northern-based studio.

10

NORTHERN FILMS WITH NORTHERN TALENT

JOHN BLAKELEY'S FILMS were simply made and highly profitable. His film studio in London was a modest set-up over a garage. And he kept everything simple – plots, camera work, editing.

It was against this background that he launched so many acts who had made a name in theatre and on radio on a film career that was to bring them national acclaim.

Among them was George Formby, whose first two movies were *Boots Boots* and *Off the Dole*.

George Formby followed his father of the same name into show business, and after his father's death, the young George followed his act on stage, only later developing his own personal style. It was his wife, dancer Beryl Ingham, who brought the banjolele into his act and played a major role in re-shaping his career.

It is interesting to note that the first two films he made with John Blakeley started to show the move from George's character inherited from his father to the warmer, loveable character he was to become as his career progressed.

The formula of providing popular comedies that could be enjoyed by everyone provided a real boost during and after the war years, as audiences who were in desperate need of something to lift them out of the gloom flocked to see them.

A number of these comedies brought legendary comic Frank Randle to the screen, which was something of a coup for John Blakeley. Randle was the highest paid comic in the country at the time.

Frank Randle was born Arthur Hughes in Wigan, changing his name to Arthur McEvoy when his mother married.

From a young age, he loved to entertain holidaymakers on the beach at Blackpool, where he eventually went to live. He got his first break in show business when he joined an acrobatic team as a tumbler and juggler. But his first love was always comedy, for which he had a rare talent, and inevitably, after a couple more name changes, including Arthur Twist and Arthur Heath, he became a full time comedian and changed his name to Frank Randle.

By the time he signed his film contract with John Blakeley, he was undoubtedly at the top of his profession. He had his own touring revue, *Randle's Scandals,* and was earning up to a thousand pounds a week.

He went on to make seven films for the company.

In 1947, John Blakeley finally fulfilled his ultimate ambition, to use northern talent to make northern films for northern folk in their own heartland. He transferred production from London where it had all started to Manchester, establishing his Mancunian Film Corporation studio in a disused church in Dickenson Road, Rusholme, and his biggest star, Frank Randle, was to join John Blakeley and other partners as a director of the company.

The first feature film he made there in 1948 was *Cup Tie Honeymoon* starring Yorkshire funny man Sandy Powell.

Sandy Powell was not short of experience when he made *Cup Tie Honeymoon*. He had started entertaining at a very early age and by the time he joined John Blakeley not only was he one of the best known comics in the country, but had appeared in a number of short films of his stage shows as well as in two feature films.

Cup Tie Honeymoon also featured as Sandy Powell's wife a very young Pat Phoenix, who was to go on to become one of the greatest TV sirens for over two decades as Elsie Tanner in *Coronation Street*.

And the connection with *Corrie* didn't end with Pat. The actor who played the coalman in the film was Bernard Youens, who went on to become Stan Ogden, and who, with Jean Alexander as his wife Hilda, one half of one of the most enduring double acts in British television for more than 20 years.

Pat had always wanted to be an actress, and got her first opportunity when she was 17 in *Children's Hour* for the BBC. She joined Rusholme Repertory Company, where she first worked with Bernard, and it was while they were both there that they came to the notice of John Blakeley.

The strong link between John Blakeley's film studio and the northern variety scene also resulted in the emergence on screen of another stalwart of *Corrie,* Betty Driver.

Betty had started her career with a repertory company in Longsight, Manchester, where she was spotted at the tender age of 12 by John and given a song and dance routine in the George Formby film *Boots Boots*.

By the time she was 14, she was appearing with Gracie Fields and Norman Evans, and was to go on to a very successful singing career with the big bands in the 60s, before returning to her roots as an actress and joining the cast of *Coronation Street* in 1969 as barmaid Betty Turpin, a character she was to play for more than 40 years.

During the era of Mancunian Films, John Blakeley changed the lives of many an actor and turn from the theatres as he created stars of the silver screen.

Some were at the peak of their profession, others were on their way up and have John to thank for giving them their big break and the exposure that would pave the way to their becoming international stars.

The list of names who appeared in Mancunian Films productions read like a who's who of show business.

Frank Randle, George Formby, Gracie Fields, Sandy Powell, Wee Georgie Wood, Norman Evans, Betty Driver, Pat Phoenix, Bernard Youens, Jimmy Clitheroe, Tessie O'Shea, Josef Locke. Jimmy Jewel and Ben Warris, Jimmy James, Nat Jackley and so the parade of stars goes on.

There were many radio stars of the day who the public could at last put faces to, including the stars of one of the most popular radio shows of the 40s, *Happidrome* – Cecil Frederick, who was Ramsbottom, Robbie Vincent who was Enoch and Harry Korris as Mr Lovejoy.

All these famous names. as well as established actors and actresses like Sally Barnes and Diana Dors, who was a Rank starlet but out on loan to gain more experience.

John Blakeley's dream lasted for six years. At 65 he decided to retire, and in 1953, he made his last film at the Manchester studios before selling the building to the BBC a year later.

The film was *It's a Grand Life*, and starred Frank Randle and Diana Dors.

As with the rep theatres, it was becoming increasingly apparent that television was soon going to have some effect on John's film operation.

The Mancunian Film Corporation, for many years the only feature film studio outside Greater London, made a massive contribution to the cultural life and history of entertainment in this country.

The former disused church in Manchester was to achieve another first when it became the first regional TV studio outside London, and the home of a variety of BBC programmes from *Top of the Pops* to *Grandstand* for years to come.

On John Blakeley's retirement, Mancunian Films was to continue for many more years under the direction of John's son, Tom, but now with the studios based back in London. Here they provided the facilities for making many B movies and Hammer Horror films.

The influence of John Blakeley, his family and co-directors in broadening the horizons of so many performers is immeasurable, bringing them to the screen for the first time, and bringing pleasure to thousands of cinemagoers, especially during some of the country's darkest hours.

And in so doing creating a legacy that was to play a major role in the foundation of the newly-formed ITV network just a couple of years later.

For as well as Pat Phoenix, Betty Driver, Bernard Youens, countless other actors who had worked with Mancunian Films were to turn up over the next few years, not only in *Coronation Street* but in many other roles in the numerous television dramas being produced in Manchester.

And it wasn't only on the performing side. The expertise developed by technicians with Mancunian Films was to make just as big a contribution to the formation of Granada Television. Sound engineers, cameramen, designers, lighting technicians, directors – so many had learned their craft with John Blakelely.

And the family story goes on. Mike Blakeley, grandson of the founder of the Mancunian Film Corporation, was to go on to a long and distinguished career as a cameraman with Granada TV, making a significant contribution to so many award winning programmes, eventually setting up his own studios, where the family tradition was to continue when Mike was joined by his son.

While Mike Popley, the son of Bernard Youens also went into the business to became one of GTV's most senior cameramen, too.

So, thanks to the experience they had gained with Mancunian Films, for many of those stars who had graced the stages of the music halls and repertory theatres for so many years, whose traditional venues were fast disappearing, the advent of commercial television was by no means the end of the road.

Merely a new beginning.

THE COMIC'S TALE

11

FROM THE BOARDS TO THE COBBLES

INITIALLY THE CAST of *Coronation Street* was drawn from the many performers who had been earning a living as actors, their backgrounds as varied as the characters they portrayed.

And that has been the general pattern over the many years that *Corrie* has been running. They may have started their careers in amateur dramatics groups, rep companies, theatre workshops, youth theatre or, in the case of more than one young character, joined straight from school.

Following the initial cast, who were to bring to life so vividly the concept created by Tony Warren and build the strong foundations on which *Coronation Street* was built, many were to go on to establish enduring characters who quickly became household names and have been central to the show for many years, and with whom I had the pleasure of working for so long.

And there are members of the cast who are still part of the *Corrie* legend after more than three decades with the show.

They include William Roache of course, who has been there since day one and has now played Ken Barlow for over 50 years. Eileen Derbyshire who plays Emily Bishop has been with the show for almost as long. Barbara Knox, Anne Kirkbride and Helen Worth have been making Rita, Deirdre and Gail household names for over 40 years, Sue Nicholls has played Audrey for 30 years, and there are a number of other actors who are rapidly approaching that milestone.

Such is the loyalty to the show, that there are stage crew and technicians who have been with it for almost as long.

But as the show progressed, it became not uncommon for a character to be cast not with the traditional background of an actor, but from the variety side of the business.

And some were to become established among our most successful and best loved characters.

They may have had previous experience in television or film, or had appeared in the odd stage comedy, but by and large their roots had been in variety. That was where they had made their name.

They pounded the boards week in, week out, up and down the country, Some went on to become household names through radio and later television. Some may have spent a lifetime working in variety and never get any further than supporting act.

But for many, not only did *Coronation Street* kick-start a new career at a time when most were thinking of retirement, but the show was to give them recognition beyond their wildest dreams.

A fine example of this is exactly what happened to a very good friend of mine who had been in the entertainment business for over 50 years.

He had been with *Stars in Battledress* during the war, topped the bill on radio and in variety theatres for years, had a Royal Variety performance to his credit and had appeared in a number of stage plays. He had featured in some of Granada's major drama productions and had even appeared in *Coronation Street* in minor roles.

We used to go for a drink every Thursday night, and despite his vast experience, the fact that his name had been a by-word for comedy to theatre and radio audiences for close on half a century, his appearance in whatever hostelry we happened to be gracing with our presence that week prompted not one glimmer of recognition.

Until he was cast in the role of the irascible Percy Sugden in *Coronation Street*.

The entertainer was Bill Waddington. After recording his first episode, we were having our usual Thursday night beverage. I told him that in three weeks time after that episode had hit the screens, it would change his life completely. He wouldn't be able to go into that pub or any other ever again without instant recognition.

And it was true. By then living in semi retirement, as soon as he hit the screens as Percy Sugden, he once again became an overnight national treasure.

Such is the impact of *Coronation Street*.

Many of the top post-war variety acts had started their careers with entertainment units in the armed forces during the war years, going on to reach the peak of their profession during the decade following the cessation of hostilities.

The wartime entertainment units were made up of serving Army personnel, mostly professional entertainers. They were good, there is no doubt about that. They had to be to entertain the troops under those conditions and to be able to lift their spirits.

But it became apparent after a while that such had been the proliferation of entertainment units, that some form of rationalisation had to take place. Every unit wanted to start a concert party, and quite simply there were too many of them – *Blue Pencils, Norfolk Turkeys, Thumbs Up, Mustard Pots* and so the list went on.

So a central pool of artistes was established and it was from this that *Stars in Battledress* was created by Colonel Basil Brown, Major Bill Alexander and Captain George Black, the son of impresario George Black.

Together with ENSA – Entertainment National Service Association, which was set up in 1939 by Basil Dean and Leslie Henson, they formed a crack force of entertainers who were to entertain the troops both overseas and at home throughout the war years.

During the war, there were also many radio shows to raise the morale of the public as well as the serving forces – *Ack Ack Beer Beer, Middle East Merry-Go-Round, Private Smith Entertains* and many more.

Many of the wartime radio shows continued after the war, when they were joined by numerous others, all making full use of the wide-ranging entertainment experience that had warmed the hearts and kept up the spirits of audiences during the dark years.

Middle East Merry-Go-Round became *Merry-Go-Round*, there was *John Sharman's Music Hall, Round the Halls, London Lights, Variety Bandbox,* and of course, *Blackpool Night* and *Workers Playtime*, to name but a few.

This was undoubtedly the golden age, as the entertainers who had become household names through radio during and after the war, worked the big theatres up and down the country playing to full houses, the audiences desperately hungry for anything to cheer them up and eager to put faces to the artistes they had come to know over the airwaves.

And the variety turns certainly rose to the challenge. Whether vocalists, speciality acts, musicians or comics, after what they had been through, they were undoubtedly masters of their craft.

As well as the theatres, they began to find work in the cabaret clubs that were springing up all over London in particular.

A popular venue in the capital was the Windmill Theatre managed by Vivian van Damme. The Windmill was famous for having kept its doors open throughout the duration of the war and continued to thrive as a major attraction with the return of peacetime. The theatre may not have been the easiest place to play, but it provided a first class training ground for many of the star names who became national hits during the golden years of variety.

The Windmill provided non-stop entertainment all day, six days a week. But the main attraction was the scantily-clad girls who adorned the stage. The variety turns certainly weren't the ones the audience had paid to see. They used to go on between the girls' acts, and if they could manage to hold the audience in those circumstances, they were good. No doubt about it.

As a result, some of the greatest names in entertainment would probably have had some experience of the Windmill, and all would agree it was one of the greatest groundings they could have had on the way to the peak of their chosen profession.

One of the comic's biggest problems was protecting his act. The more successful he became, the more difficult the task.

In this respect, radio could be a double-edged sword. On the one hand, it was great to do because it gave the performer national recognition and put up his box office appeal no end. But success on radio, or later, television, which led to an even wider audience, brought its problems. The old turns had to do a lot more work on their acts.

Before they became stars of broadcasting, they could have got away with working the same act from one end of the country to the other. A string of gags, a couple of funny ditties, with perhaps the odd adjustment to take in some local reference to the different venues, particularly in pantomime or a seaside summer season, could keep them going for months.

The act could stay the same because as the venues changed, so did the audience. But a radio broadcast would change all that.

One of the biggest shows on radio was *Blackpool Night,* which was recorded at the Jubilee Theatre in front of a live audience, and without doubt one of the most famous voices in those days was that of Jack Watson, who introduced the show.

And there was eventually to be a *Coronation Street* connection there, as Jack during his long acting career eventually played one of Elsie's Tanner's boyfriends, Bill Gregory.

It was every comic's dream to appear on *Blackpool Night.* But once he'd used a gag in a show like that, it was over and done with. Once the performance had been broadcast, that was it. The hunt for new material became a serious matter.

And that wasn't the only consideration. Once a gag had reached such a wide audience, the comic could put money on it turning up sooner or later in someone else's act.

Gag thieves, they were known as. And they didn't confine their activities to what they heard on radio or picked up from television.

They would be just as bare-faced about it in the theatres. They were acts notorious for pinching gags. And they became well known to the pros, particularly during a summer season.

The gag thieves would turn up at everyone else's show and make notes. During their run they would feed the gags into their own act. And they were cheeky, with it.

One comic was doing a Sunday night special in a seaside town where he'd performed many times before and was hugely popular. But on this occasion he had a very lukewarm reception. He couldn't understand it – until the stage manager told him that the week before they'd had a comic on the bill who'd done his act virtually word for word.

It turned out to be a young comic learning the business, who had appeared on the same bill as the seasoned performer some time before. The old hand, in a gesture to help the newcomer, had given him some of his wartime gags and a few pointers as to how to work an audience.

The youngster had repaid him by pinching virtually his whole act!

Bill Waddington recalled spotting one young comic in the audience making notes. It was obvious what he was up to.

He even had the cheek to go and see Bill afterwards and say how much he'd enjoyed his act.

'I wish I'd told half your gags,' he said.

'You will,' said Bill.

He met him in a bar a couple of days later. He was looking through his loose change. He spotted Bill and called across to him.

'Have you got a tanner. I want to phone a friend.'

Bill gave him two and told him to phone them all!

The seaside landladies could be the staunchest allies of the summer season pro. If they recommended your show to their guests, it was the best publicity you could get. It could make the difference between a full theatre and half empty. They were invited to most shows and knew who did what. And if they came across someone who pinched another act's gags, they would get no help in filling their theatre from the landladies.

Before he went into *Coronation Street*, Bill Waddington had been performing in theatres for over half a century.

He took his first tentative steps into showbusiness at the tender age of 12 when he entertained the regulars in his father's pub in Oldham when the comedian who had been booked failed to turn up.

He had appeared in pantomime, comedy plays, farces, but he had made his reputation as a stand-up comic, topping the bill up and down the country, always finishing with a little ditty as he accompanied himself on his ukulele proclaiming that he was 'Witty Willie and I come from Lancashire'.

Before he appeared as Percy Sugden in *Coronation Street*, Bill had previously played five minor roles in the show. He recalled the first one being an old man with a pipe in the Rovers who just had to sit there until Stan Ogden told a joke, then laugh and walk out.

When we were looking for another elderly character with plenty to say for himself, his name came to mind immediately to more than one writer, not solely because of his role as the old man with the pipe, I should point out.

He had appeared in a number of roles in other drama series, including *Fallen Hero* and *Family at War*, but his big break into television had come when he appeared in Peter Eckersley's production of Victoria Wood's *Talent* for Granada Television.

So he was brought in to *Corrie* to create the role of the indefatigable Percy.

He brought a new dimension to the Street and a wealth of comedy experience that was to influence many storylines, as did so many entertainers from the world of variety and clubland who were to follow him onto the most famous cobbled street in the world.

12

FROM A FACTORY NEAR YOU

ONE OF THE most popular radio shows in the 1950s and 1960s was *Workers Playtime*. It started as a wartime programme, and carried on for a long time afterwards.

It was a thirty-minute variety show broadcast live daily at lunchtime on location from factories all over the country. The warmth and enthusiasm shown by the audiences in the works canteen was spontaneous and genuine, as they welcomed some of the biggest stars of the day.

One of the first radio sketches I ever sold was for *Workers Playtime* – to a little known double act called Morecambe and Wise.

When I am recounting my experiences to a handful of members of the local Flower Club and Allotments Society (in return for a rich tea biscuit and a cup of tea, if the kettle is working) I like to tell those who are still awake and listening that it was a turning point for all of us.

'Morecambe and Wise went on to become one of the most famous, funniest and best loved double acts of all time – and who'd have thought I'd have been stood here talking to you tonight!'

But *Workers Playtime* could prove a testing time for those who appeared on it.

It wasn't like performing in a working men's club where the act could be fighting for the attention of the audience whose focus could be anywhere but on the turn as they eagerly antici-pated the arrival of the pies or the raffle draw.

The audience would be eating in the canteen from where

the show was broadcast, but the atmosphere was friendly, welcoming and intimate. The comics would make full use of this informality, getting a laugh or two out of what the factory was producing, find out the names of some of the personalities who worked there and take the mickey out of them. They would have a go at the foreman, any other character who was well known in the factory for whatever reason – anything they could latch on to. And the audience loved it.

But it wasn't just a matter of turning up and churning out any old material. The show may be coming from a string factory in Yorkshire, which employed no more than a hundred or so people, but it was being broadcast on national radio. Apart from the localised patter, the rest of the material all had to be fresh.

And because of the nature of the show and the fact that it was all broadcast live, there were times when scheduled artistes couldn't make it at the last minute.

When that happened, a replacement had to be found at very short notice, usually someone working locally who was within easy reach of the venue.

Under those circumstances, it wasn't unusual for the turns to be making up the script as they drove to the factory!

But it was never a problem. The majority had an encyclopaedic store of gags for every occasion filed away in their memories. If they had an audience, no matter how big or small, there was no way they were going to disappoint. It would take more than a canteen full of hungry factory workers to knock a top turn out of his stride.

Blackpool was undoubtedly regarded as the glittering jewel in the crown of British seaside entertainment. Where so many gags first saw the light of day, as the acts working the theatres in the evenings spent every spare moment looking for material in every situation.

And where so many variety acts strove to get on the bill for a summer season, even if their name was initially so far down the bill that they could have been mistaken for the printer.

The bill was very important. The running order dictated the pace, flavour and general tone of the show and could spell box office success or disaster.

Hitting on the right mix, the right order of appearance of your dancers, comics, speciality acts, musicals was all important, as was the running time. It had to be right. It could make or break a show.

A variety show may typically run for one hour and forty five minutes, with an interval. I once asked a theatre manager how long the interval was in his show. He replied: 'As long as the ice cream queue!'

The acts each had their own allotted time, and to stick to it was crucial to the smooth running of the show. I have even heard of managements who refused to re-book acts who went over, deeming them as 'unreliable', though I can't think this ever applied to a certain Mr Ken Dodd, in my opinion and I am sure of everyone who has seen him, not only the finest stand-up comedian of his generation but in terms of the laughter generated, probably the best of all time.

It didn't apply to every theatre management. Many worked on the maxim that if the show was going well, the audience were enjoying themselves, let it run. And if they thought they were getting better value for money than the first house audience, so much the better.

This policy didn't always go down well with the stage crew, though. They wanted to get home at night, and I heard of one closing act, a singer/pianist, who after running over for every performance was about to go into his final number one night when he was suddenly confronted by the stage door keeper who slapped a bunch of keys onto the piano and told him to lock up when he had finished!

The pattern for the top stars was summer season, touring provincial theatres, pantomime, touring again, then back to summer season, with countless radio broadcasts thrown in.

Life for a variety act was nomadic, to say the least. They would work from Monday to Saturday, travel on Sunday and open in another theatre the following day, sometimes at the other end of the country. This is how Crewe Station came to take its place in the folklore of the variety theatre. All journeys seemed to change at Crewe, and many acts looked forward to catching up on the latest news and gossip from their friends as their paths briefly crossed en route to their next venue.

So when they got to pantomime or to summer season, for the top turns it was a chance to escape for a while from the rigorous routine of another week, another town, another theatre.

Many of them made it a real home from home by renting a house for the duration of their run. For one thing, it was cheaper than digs but the real bonus was that they could have their families with them. Their children would go to local schools, and it was as near as some of them came to anything approaching any sort of 'normal' family life.

Of course, there were many acts who never did become household names, and struggled from one date to the next, barely making a living.

But few ever gave up. They never gave up the notion that they were pros, even if for them the peak of success would be working in a summer concert party in a park or on a sea front.

And not many of those who did make it big ever forgot their roots. They never forgot what a struggle it had been to make ends meet.

One well-known comic who was never out of work summer or winter and was one of the best panto dames in the business, used to tell how he was kept in short pants until he was eighteen just so his dad could get half price for him on the train.

His dad had been as successful as he was, but he never forgot those days when every penny counted.

13

A FUNNY THING HAPPENED

THE COMIC WAS always on the look out for the funny side of any situation, remark or conversation.

'That was the raw material of our craft,' Bill Waddington told me as we reminisced about his glittering career in variety.

And there was certainly no shortage of that. That was in the days when the sun shone all summer and Blackpool was in its heyday. There would be so many people on the sands, the tide had to wait for them all to go back to their digs for their tea before it could come in.

'The comic would get a gag out of any situation, any overheard conversation.'

And the women gave him plenty of opportunity, as they chatted among themselves.

Quite often, they would be in twos or threes, while their husbands were renewing old friendships and cultivating new ones over a lunchtime session in the pub.

It may be two women sat in deck chairs:

'What sort of a place have you got, then?'
'Nice room, Very handy. Right next door to the doings.'
'Is yours all right?'
'Food's good. Fish and chips, egg and chips, sausage and chips. We can have chips on their own if we want.'
'I'm pleased you're suited. By the way, I hope you don't mind me mentioning it, but what have you done to your hair? It looks like a wig.'
'It is a wig.'
'Really. Isn't that marvellous.'

'*Nobody would ever know.*'

Or out of an overheard discussion between a couple of women waiting for a tram, when one was trying to explain to her friend with some difficulty how an insurance policy worked.

This woman in next street insured her husband's life for £300.

As the insurance man drove off, he ran over her dearly beloved.

So he went back into the house and told the widow what he had done.

'*Eeh, that didn't take long,*' *she said.* '*I'll go and get your £300.*'

The gag would come out of any situation. There was a well-known spot in Blackpool favoured by ladies of easy virtue.

I was waiting for my missus outside the hairdressers. While I was standing there, one of those ladies came up to me and asked me if I was looking for a good time. Because if I was, she could show me one. For £10.

I told her she was wasting her time. I only had a pound.

'*A pound,*' *she said.* '*You'll not get much for that..*'

Half an hour later, I was walking along the front with my missus. Just had her hair done. Looking a million dollars, she was, when I come across this lady of easy virtue again.

She took one look at my missus and shouted across: '*I told you wouldn't get much for a pound.*'

There was no shortage of fresh fish stalls in Blackpool. These were always good for a gag.

My pal was walking along the front with a lobster he'd just bought, when he met a friend of his.

He looked at the lobster.

'*Are you taking it home for tea?*'

'No,' he said 'He's had his tea. We're off to the pictures.'

Then there was the lady who went up to a fish stall on the front and picked up a crab.

'Are these crabs fresh?' she asked.

'Fresh, madam? Half an hour ago, that one you've got in your hand came out of the sea, walked across the promenade and jumped up onto that slab.'

She sniffed the crab and put it back.

'I think it must have trod in something on the way.'

Another gag came to mind one day standing on the promenade near North Pier as the tide went out.

Wife's nephew came to Blackpool last week. He'd walked all the way from Wigan. He'd never been to the seaside before. When he got here, the tide was in. His feet were killing him. He said to this feller next to him 'I'd love to soak my feet in a bucket of that.'

'I can arrange that,' he said 'Ten bob a bucket.'

'I'll be right back,' said the lad.

So he walked all the way back to Wigan, got his ten bob, and walked all the way back. By the time he got back, the tide had gone out.

'By heck,' he said. 'You've been doing a roaring trade. If I'd been much longer you'd have sold out'!

Or out of watching two men hiring a boat to go out fishing.

It was nearly time to go back, and they hadn't caught a thing. Suddenly they were surrounded by fish, practically throwing themselves in the boat.

'Just our luck,' said Frank. 'We've got to take the boat back.'

'We'll come back tomorrow,' said Ernie.

'But we'll not be able to find this spot again,' said Frank.

'Yes, we will', said Ernie.

'I'll put a cross on the back of the boat so we'll know where to come.'

'*That's no good*' said Frank.

'*We might not get this boat tomorrow.*'

The minds of the comics never stopped working, and they would get a gag out of almost any situation.

Wives were prime targets for their humour, whether they were married or not. Most of the audience were, and that's all that mattered.

'*My wife's housebound, you know*'.

'*I'm sorry to hear that. How long has she been like that?*'

'*Since I tied her up and left her in the kitchen.*'

And so they went on. The routines were seemingly endless.

When I finished my first week's work, I handed my pay packet over to the missus.

'*Here,*' *she said.* '*Here's something for your pocket*'.

And she gave me a handkerchief.

The audiences loved them, and the more outrageous they became, the better.

I asked Bill if his wife ever took exception to what he had to say about her.

'No' he said. 'She knew I had two wives – my real missus, and my stage wife, the one I tell the stories about'.

There was even a smile to be got out of the serious business of income tax.

I went to see the tax man this morning. He said he'd noticed I was claiming expenses for the wife.

He said if I stayed in a hotel during the course of my work, that was business. But if I took the wife along, that was pleasure.

I said '*Pleasure? Have you seen my wife?*'

He lost his appeal!

14

HAVE YOU A GOOD MEMORY FOR FACES?

THERE WERE A thousand and one gags spawned by seaside landladies.

Most visitors stayed in boarding houses. They could all relate to landlady stories. And this was one thing the comic usually had in common with his audience.

If the landlady was as bad as the comic made out, he was sharing an experience with the holidaymaker. If they had good landladies, they laughed out of a sense of relief that they didn't have the one they were hearing about.

This was ideal territory for patter comics like Bill – those who didn't tell jokes, but pattered on about situations. Painted pictures with words.

The landlady was no oil painting. But give her her due, she did like to make the best of herself. She was having a shave when we arrived.

I thought it was going to be a posh place when I walked in.

Even the rat holes had revolving doors.

But things are never as they seem, are they?

'Now young man, I've given you a nice room on the top floor. You can see the sea'.

'Through the window?'

'No. Through the hole in the roof.'

I said 'Do I have running water in my room?'

'Certainly,' she said.

And she was right. It was running down the walls.

She said 'Have you got a good memory for faces?'
I asked her why she was asking.
'There's no mirror in the bathroom.'
We came down on the first morning, there was a kipper nailed to the wall with a notice. 'Wipe your bread on here.'
That was breakfast.

'The secret was for the comic to keep his material on familiar ground so the audience would quickly identify with it', said Bill.

I was coming past Central Station, when I met this chap struggling with this great big suitcase. I said 'I'll give you a hand with that.'

Well I think he had the kitchen sink in there. I struggled and strained for half an hour before we got to where he was stopping. 'Thanks very much,' he said 'Do you smoke?' I told him I did, and waited for the tip. He said 'I thought you did. Way you were huffing and puffing up that hill. I'd give it up if I were you.'

This sort of thing went down well with the audiences because most of them staying in digs were familiar with Central Station in Blackpool. It was where most of them arrived. They were also familiar with the trek to their digs, hauling their luggage along with them.

So they could relate to every aspect of the story.

It was part of the entertainer's craft to know the audiences and work to them.

Glasgow Empire was known, not without good reason, as the graveyard of many an English comic. Not all of them, granted. But given a choice, many comics from the North of England would rather have had all their teeth out.

So they didn't go there. But they couldn't stop Glasgow coming to them – particularly when it came to Scots fortnight in Blackpool. So the first thing to do, was get the audience on your side – if you could do that, you were at least in with a fighting chance.

So it had to be funny, feature the Scots, and make the comic the butt of the humour. Bill recalled one story that encompassed all three beautifully.

It concerned Angus, who went down to London for the first time in his life. When he came back, his mates asked him how he went on.

'Och, I've never come across such terrible people. I'm never going there again. Ranting, raving, screaming kicking on my door at three o'clock in the morning.'

'That's awful, Angus. What did you do?'

'I took no notice. I just carried on playing my bagpipes.'

Not every entertainer topped the bill in a seaside summer season. The majority had to be happy with lesser venues.

When I was working on the local paper, I went to a theatre club to interview a speciality act, Chief Geronimo.

Dressed for the part in feathered headdress and buckskin suit, he threw knives into a board in front of which stood his girl assistant holding balloons. The aim was to burst the balloons and by the grace of God and much to the relief of his assistant, he seemed to achieve it without mishap to her, himself or the audience, who in some cases were far too close to the action for comfort. This was before Health and Safety had been invented, I might add.

The only danger he saw in the act, though his assistant wouldn't agree, was to himself because with having a lot of time on his hands during the day, he spent too much of it eating, which together with lack of exercise and a forty a day habit, was putting his health at some considerable risk.

But by the end of the week Chief Geronimo – surprise, surprise, that wasn't his real name but it did fit the act better than Reginald Furnival – had discovered the elixir of life.

Apparently, the secret of good health that would not only reduce his girth to manageable proportions and some semblance of fitness, but achieve it without him having to resort to anything resembling physical exercise, had been given to him over a drink in the bar by a well-meaning member of the audience who claimed to be in the nutrition business.

And what was this magic potion? Pureed turnip.

So he went on a pureed turnip diet. He was assured he would soon acquire a taste for it, and most importantly it would get his weight down quicker than anything.

And it did. I heard some weeks later that he had been taken to hospital suffering from malnutrition!

15

HOW DO YOU LIKE YOUR STEAK BOILED?

Every seaside entertainer had an endless fund of stories of theatre digs, some good, some bad and some quite horrendous.

To say that some of them did not quite come up to expectations was an understatement – and that was being polite.

One top of the bill variety act recalled: 'When I went somewhere I'd never been before and they opened the door, if I could smell cats or gas, I was off.'

'I'd come up with some sort of excuse, but I wouldn't stop there.'

'We all had a fund of reasons, but my most convincing was when I told them some friends of mine had turned up at the theatre, and if I didn't go and stay with them, they'd be very upset.'

Many acts preferred digs to a hotel, though they could well afford to stay in one. They would get more privacy. And people who ran theatrical digs were generally very understanding people, They loved the theatre and they were very attentive.

'When would you like your meals? Anything special we can do for you?'

Not everyone, mind. Some places were quite disgusting. The rooms would be damp, kitchens filthy, food practically inedible, linen unwashed.

Many an old pro would take up running theatrical digs, and the majority were fine. It was good to renew old acquaintances. But unless you knew where you were going, it may not have been the best place to be. They'd be keen to tell you what they'd done in their careers. Each night they'd take you through their life story and that was the last thing you wanted when you finished work after two houses.

So when the entertainers found somewhere good to stay, they would go back every time they were in town.

And if they were told there was no room that week, some of them would go to great lengths to ensure that there was.

When one turn was told that his chosen digs was fully booked, he would ask the landlady conversationally if she had anyone staying there that he may know. He would stop her when she came to a certain name – who it was didn't matter – and say how surprised he was to hear that he was coming back, after what he had said about the place last time.

Feigning reluctance to disclose something that had been told in confidence, it was time to play the waiting game. And if the ploy had worked, it wasn't unknown for some poor innocent to get a phone call from the landlady saying she was sorry, she wouldn't be able to accommodate him after all, while the perpetrator of the 'crime' waited for his phone to ring to be told there was now an unexpected vacancy.

It wasn't only the acts who could be choosy when it came to theatrical digs. Some landladies could be equally selective in who they took into their homes. There were endless stories of landladies who barred certain acts – no jugglers, hypnotists or animal acts. Many were deeply suspicious of dancers, particularly from the same show as another act staying there at the same time.

'There'll be no hanky panky under my roof,' she would warn sternly. But inevitably, love or lust would find a way!

And I have heard of more than one theatrical digs where if there were actors staying there, they would have cloths on the tables for their meals and the best crockery and cutlery, while the turns had to make do with bare table tops and a cracked mug or two.

But however homely the digs may be, not all landladies were skilled in every aspect of their craft.

One comic told me of a place he used to stay which was very clean, very comfortable and very accommodating. Unfortunately, the landlady wasn't the best cook in the world.

One day, he decided to treat himself. He bought some Jersey Royal potatoes, a nice piece of fillet steak and some asparagus tips.

Before he went to the theatre, he tried to tell the landlady how he wanted his evening meal cooking, but she insisted she knew exactly how he liked things.

When he returned, she had his supper ready.

She said proudly 'I've mashed your potatoes, I've boiled your meat – and your bluebells are in a vase on the piano!'

In the days when variety was the byword in the theatres, there were many speciality acts who would do anything to entertain – comics, singers, impressionists, tumblers, acrobats, trapeze artistes, wire walkers, skaters, unicyclists, jugglers, magicians, knife throwers and novelty musicians playing everything from a hose pipe to a kettle.

Some were extremely spectacular acts who usually provided breathtaking finales to their shows, like Curry's waterfalls who used to flood the stage with cascading fountains, or one man I recall finishing his act by filling the stage with flags.

There were budgies pulling little carts, dogs dressed in suits walking on their hind legs carrying umbrellas, and chickens that could count.

Others were even more bizarre. An American comic used to open by running onto the stage and falling straight into the orchestra pit.

Needless to say, he spent more time in hospital being treated for concussion than he did on stage. I don't think his career was long enough for him to become an established household name.

All very clever and entertaining in their own way. But by the time ITV came on the scene, with its big name glossy acts from both sides of the Atlantic, the big question was how much longer were the public prepared to pay to see Winnie the Wonder Dog or Charlie the Talking Cockerel?

They wanted to see the big star names they were watching on television, and there was no doubt that the days of the bizarre speciality act were definitely limited.

16

OH NO HE ISN'T. OH YES HE IS!

Pantomime played a big part in the life of an entertainer, providing work for anything from three weeks up to three months at a time of year when summer season was just a distant memory, or far ahead on the horizon.

Pantomime arrived in England in the 16th century, having probably originated in its earliest form in ancient Greece, taking its name from the single masked dancer Pantomimus. The style and content of modern pantomime has clearly defined links with a form of popular theatre in Italy in the early middle ages, when artistes would travel from province to province, improvising and telling stories at fairgrounds and in market places.

But pantomime did not find favour with everyone. It was originally considered to be a low form of opera, and only started to become popular in its own right when it found its own identity, helped in no small way by the efforts of an actor/manager by the name of John Rich. His pantomimes gradually became more topical, more comic, and in many respects more bizarre, featuring as many special theatrical effects as he could incorporate.

British pantomimes today have plots that are well tried and tested. They are broadly based on traditional children's stories, incorporating song, dance, slapstick, in-jokes and all-round over-the-top comedy and buffoonery.

But they still rigorously maintain certain conventions. Principal girl; principal boy, the leading male sometimes played by a girl; the dame, usually played by a man; villain;

good fairy; solo comic; comic double act; comic horse or cow played by two actors; a cat, a goose or some other creature played by one actor; risqué double entendre; and that all-important ingredient, audience participation.

The convention of having men play women, and women play men is thought by many to have its roots in the old festival of Twelfth Night, when it was customary for the natural order of things to be reversed.

Another suggestion is that the convention of a man playing the old woman came about because no young actress would want to make herself look that old and bizarre.

While the convention of the good fairy always entering from the right side of the stage and the villain entering from the left, is based in Commedia Dell'Arte, when the right hand side of the stage represented heaven and the left hand side represented hell.

Another popular pantomime tradition is the celebrity guest star. This can be traced back to the 19th century, when male and female impersonators were particularly popular turns.

An interesting aspect of pantomime after the war and during the following two decades, and in some cases, way beyond, were the number of double acts who really came into their own.

The business of cross talking comics started back in Victorian times with the seaside concert parties and minstrel shows, usually with the comic interrupting the MC.

Many double acts had flourished in the wartime concert parties. The routine of one performer playing the straight man with the other one sending him up scoring comic points at his expense, went down very well with the forces as they equated to the squaddie and superior officer scenario.

Maybe there was a similar psychology, the underdog using comedy to triumph over pomp, in the working men's clubs after the war, because many double acts who went on to achieve national fame started there.

And radio certainly played a big part. There was a great demand for comedy to lift the spirits of a war-torn nation, and the double act brought variety to the listener who heard not one voice but two or in some cases more, bringing variety and a change of pace to the show.

After the war, the double acts who had proved so popular as forces entertainers, both in the field and on radio, went on to enjoy massive success in the theatres, where the general public had, in many cases, the chance to see them in person for the first time.

They really were a star attraction and for some time an example of the nearest thing to full employment in their business – a long summer season, followed by four or five weeks in a top-rated pantomime in a big city venue.

For the double act, there are so many choice roles in pantomime – ugly sisters, Chinese policemen, robbers, kidnappers, broker's men, pirates.

There have been all kinds of partnerships – two girls, such as Elsie and Doris Waters (sisters of Jack Warner, a prime example of a wartime entertainer who successfully made the transition to television drama when he created the role of *Dixon of Dock Green*); Ethel Revnell and Gracie West; husband and wife teams such as Arthur Lucan and Kitty McShane, who immortalised Old Mother Riley and her daughter Kitty; and latterly Ian and Janette Tough with their ever-popular Krankies to name but a few.

There have been so many durable comic double acts over the years who became household names and it would have been unthinkable to mention one without the other. One of the longest running partnerships, which started in the 1930s, was that of cousins Jimmy Jewel and Ben Warris. They were to go on topping the bill for some 30 years, before they decided to call it a day and each pursue his own solo career.

Hope and Keen were cousins, too. Gordon and Bunny Jay, Mike and Bernie Winters were brothers – all double acts whose names were constantly on theatre bills and television shows, where for years it was most unlikely to think of one without the other.

There were many others who had come up the hard way through working men's clubs before getting their big break into television which catapulted them right to the peak of their success.

These included Cannon and Ball, Little and Large and, of course, the doyen of all double acts who came to epitomise and define for all time the very description, Eric Morecambe and Ernie Wise. They became a double act in the 1940s and continued for the next forty years, along the way collecting just about every plaudit and award going, especially after their television debut.

From the 1970s until Eric's untimely death in 1984 they could be relied on to top the television ratings whenever they appeared. One of their shows was watched by over 28 million viewers, and Christmas would not have been Christmas without Eric and Ernie. Thanks to television archives, it is a massive and truly fitting tribute that even today, almost 30 years after Eric's passing, they still provide a frequent treat for millions through repeats of their most popular shows.

One of my favourite double acts, not in the true sense of the term, as they worked together only occasionally, each having bill-topping careers on their own account, was the inimitable partnership of Cissie and Ada, better known as Les Dawson and Roy Barraclough.

The pair first aired the Cissie and Ada partnership when they were both appearing in different shows at Yorkshire

Television. Individually they were two of the finest pantomime dames in the business.

Les, of course was one of the country's funniest, multi-talented entertainers, while Roy is an actor of remarkable depth. As well as his well-known stint in *Coronation Street* playing Alec Gilroy, Roy is a stage performer of great experience, giving us writers not only a wealth of comedy talent but a vast range of performance to exploit.

Whether he was doing a comic routine as part of the Cissie and Ada act with Les Dawson, playing pantomime dame, working in serious drama, much of it at his much-loved Bolton Octagon theatre, or carrying the wide range between comedy and pathos that his *Coronation Street* role of Alec Gilroy demanded, Roy is always the true professional, totally reliable in whatever he is doing.

And when he and Les did get together, anyone privileged to be in their company was in for a real treat – a 24 carat nugget of pure, spontaneous comedy from two men who just could not seem to help sparking off each other.

We first met Les at a Press Ball in Manchester. I never knew him to turn down any request to attend a charity function, if it was at all possible.

He was a quiet, small figure at the corner of the bar, until my wife joined me, when he suddenly pulled his Cosmo Smallpiece specs from his pocket, narrowed his eyes, practically engulfed his nose with his bottom lip and uttered those time honoured words 'Knickers, knackers, knockers' as he leered at her.

When she got over the shock and realised it was Les, she found him to be the charming, caring man we were to come to know. We met Les and his wife Tracy on several occasions at Granada TV functions.

Les's talents were legend and went far beyond comedy.

As well as his hilarious stand-up routines, his piano playing, game show host, including his unforgettable stint with *Blankety Blank* and being one of the best pantomime dames in the business, he was a brilliant writer, too, as anyone who has read any of his novels will testify. It is probably not one of the better-known aspects of this multi-talented entertainer that he wrote upwards of a dozen novels.

His untimely death robbed the entertainment world of a true giant of variety.

I feel privileged that my life has been touched and greatly enriched by knowing and working with so many talented people, whose sole aim in their lives has been to entertain.

17

WHEN IMPROVISATION SHOULD CARRY A HEALTH WARNING

PANTOMIME HAS ALWAYS been special, and if it went well, it could be a long season. And if it was a big hit with the audiences and the box office tills were jingling, it wasn't unusual for the performers to find themselves doing a dozen shows or more a week.

For the dame, it could be very physically demanding. To have six or more costume changes in one performance was not unusual.

With such a long run, the performers were always looking for ways to make it more interesting, not only for the audience but for themselves. There is a lot of improvisation in pantomime. They were always thinking of new bits of business from day to day, much of it never coming to light until the actual performance where it appeared.

And if it totally threw the rest of the company for a minute or two, so much the better. The cast loved it – and so did the audience.

And the stars loved to involve the audience, especially the children.

But one old pro who had played his part in delighting panto audiences for close on forty years as musical director was adamant that one of the first lessons to be learned was never to throw anything into the audience – even with the best of intentions.

It was a lesson that was brought home to him fairly early on in his career, when he was working as musical director on *Cinderella* in Liverpool.

Early in the second half, Buttons would involve one or two of the kids from the audience. He'd pick some volunteers to go up on to the stage, get them to sing a daft song, and they'd go off with a chocolate bar.

There was one young comic doing his first panto playing Baron Hardup's flunky – 'not much money but great for the experience' he was told when offered the part. He loved every minute. And once he'd got his confidence and begun to enjoy himself, he thought it would be good to involve a few more of the kids himself.

And he knew exactly how he would do it.

He had a slapstick scene. His normal routine was to end it by tripping with a bucket, the contents of which instead of being water was confetti. He threw this out over the first couple of rows of the audience, end of scene.

But at this particular matinee performance he had the idea of taking in some sweets, so the bucket wasn't filled with confetti. It contained something with much more appeal to the young audience.

He hadn't told the rest of the cast of his plan. If he had, there was no way they would have gone along with it. They would have known where it was all going to end.

It all went according to plan and they moved on to the next scene, a front of cloth piece between the ugly sisters as the crew cleared up the stage and the kids in the first half dozen rows scrabbled about between the seats, hunting down the sweets.

But they had no intention of eating them. As soon as the wicked baron made his next entrance, as well as being greeted by the usual hissing and booing, back came the sugar-coated missiles.

All he could do was take cover until the barrage had finished. Appeals for them to stop, only made it worse.

The throwing of sweets into the audience was never repeated, but it didn't stop the missiles. The kids must have told their mates, because at the next performance they were bringing their own missiles – anything from liquorice allsorts to acorns, conkers and apples.

The orchestra played the rest of the run under a net!

When the turns were in summer season or pantomime, they became part of the community.

Just like the rep actors, they belonged to the town. The town belonged to them.

But however well known he was, if a comic was playing in pantomime, the star name disappeared. As soon as the curtain went up, he became Buttons, or Idle Jack, or Simple Simon. That's the way the kids saw it and that's the way it had to be.

This accounted for the way that many star turns eventually found renewed fame as character actors. As one top of the bill variety star told me: 'You've got to be able to act to perform. Telling gags is acting. If you're telling a story about a little old man or a little old woman, you look at it from their point of view. You have to if you're going to make it convincing. All good comedy has a root in reality, no matter how far you stretch it ultimately.'

'If you can stand up on stage for half an hour and make people laugh, re-enact all those character parts you are talking about, you can act. No doubt about that.'

'Consequently, it wasn't that difficult to do a play. Playing a role instead of playing the comic was no problem. You just played the role.'

'If it was a good story and had a destination, it would work for you.'

When they were in summer season, the stars would likely do two houses a night, with matinees on Wednesday and Saturday. If it was wet at mid-day, they may put on an extra matinee – but never in Blackpool. There wasn't much point. There were too many other attractions, the biggest being the Tower.

Most folk took their holidays from Saturday to Saturday. The worst house of the week was first house on a Friday.

They were coming to the end of their holidays. They had settled their bills and were going home the next day.

Saturday night wasn't generally so good, either. Those who could be bothered going to the shows at all were usually tired after the travelling.

The beginning of the week was best, because the visitors by then had settled in, had most of their holiday to look forward to and weren't even thinking of going home.

The shows never changed. Even when there were three performances a day, the turns would rarely change a word.

Folk who were on holiday for two weeks would probably go twice, and expect to see the same show. They'd often take along someone else. If they knew what was coming up, it would make them feel a bit special, in the know. They would feel a part of the show.

For many holidaymakers, it was the only time they went to the theatre from one year's end to the next. But on holiday they didn't need much persuading. They would eagerly turn up to see in the flesh the turns who had become so familiar through radio and television.

And if you didn't go to see a summer show, you would find yourself virtually a social outcast in your digs. There was no more popular topic of conversation over breakfast than the show folk had seen the night before.

18

THE NUTS AND BOLTS OF VARIETY

OVER THE YEARS there have been many turns appearing as characters in *Coronation Street* who have covered just about the whole spectrum of the entertainment business – radio, variety theatre, pantomime, from chorus girls and dancers to speciality acts and stand-up comics, from forces concert party, the Windmill Theatre to the West End stage.

And many of them were no strangers to the working men's club circuit in the north of England.

Working men's clubs were originally founded in the 19th century in industrial areas of the country, particularly the north of England, with the aim of providing recreation and education for working class men and their families.

But despite the educational aims of the founders, working men's clubs quickly became purely recreational with bars, snooker tables, food and entertainment. It was in this environment that many of our top entertainers cut their teeth.

Most of the working men's clubs are affiliated to the Working Men's Club and Institute Union, which was founded in 1862, and such affiliation for many became almost a badge of approval. Hence the words of introduction from countless concert secretaries: 'Welcome to the Barnsdyke (or wherever) Working Men's Club – affiliated.'

The notion that working the northern clubs was a glamorous life was not exactly endorsed by the majority of acts.

If you were a big name, top of the bill, and you went on after everyone had eaten, after they'd drawn the raffle and taken names for the next coach trip, you had a chance of grabbing the attention of the audience. And you could get extremely well paid for it.

But for the vast majority, it was hard work. One relentless grind.

I was playing in a charity golf tournament with a keyboard player who was one half of a musical duo. His partner, the drummer, was laid up. He had damaged his back moving equipment.

He told me that to make a living, they would play two, at times three, venues a night. And as they travelled from place to place, they had to cart with them all their equipment – keyboard, amplifiers and a full set of drums – setting it all up at each one. It was during this laborious process that the drummer had put his back out.

It was a risk they took every time they performed. But there was no way they would have given it up. That was their life. They knew no other, or wanted it. Bad backs were an occupational hazard, and that was that.

Obviously, to stay in hotels was out of the question for many acts. Decent bed and breakfasts could be expensive, so whenever possible they would stay with relatives, friends, friends of relatives, relatives of friends – anywhere to keep the cost down. And many a touring act would have a touring caravan, or a modest motor caravan, which they would set up as close to the venue as they could.

One comic who lived such a life told me of the time he pulled into a deserted market car park in a Lancashire town close on midnight on a Saturday night having been booked to appear at the theatre in a Sunday night special the following day.

It seemed an ideal spot. Town centre, close to the theatre where he was booked, and perhaps most important, but a short walk to very acceptable toilet and washing facilities.

He was awakened the next morning by what seemed to him like the sound of a football crowd outside. He drew back the curtains to find himself in the middle of the local farmers market.

And there was a queue of people at the door of his caravan waiting for him to open up and start selling bacon rolls!

It is true to say that many excellent acts who had been tirelessly working the tough club circuit for years would never have been known outside clubland but for *The Comedians* and *The Wheeltappers and Shunters Club*, two television series devised and produced by one of the most talented, respected and prolific light entertainment producers in the business, Johnnie Hamp.

Johnnie Hamp had originally worked with Granada cinemas and theatres, where he was soon showing a remarkable talent for managing stage shows and an enviable flair for the variety scene.

He became part of Granada's television operation from the outset in 1956, and he was with the company for over three decades, for much of the time as Head of Light Entertainment producing a vast array of variety shows many of them featuring top stars from both sides of the Atlantic.

The Comedians started life as an experiment in the early 1970s. Johnnie Hamp assembled a number of stand-up comics and each told gags non-stop for twenty minutes to a live audience. The results were then mixed and edited into a series of half hour shows, each featuring as many as ten or more comics.

Providing the musical sets were Shep's Banjo Boys, a seven piece band led by Howard Shepherd, and his brother Graham.

The Comedians was an instant success, and this wasn't confined to the television audience. There were sell-out national tours and even a season at the London Palladium.

One commentator saw it as a major social document of its day.

The show gave national television exposure to many club comics, turning them into household names who went on to top the bills in summer season and pantomime throughout the country for many years to come.

To mark the 40th anniversary of *The Comedians*, the man who conceived and produced that first series put together a tour featuring many of the names who had first been featured in the television version four decades earlier. It played to packed houses. There can be no greater accolade, not only to the performers but to the man who brought the whole concept to our screens in the first place – Granada TV's legendary Head of Light Entertainment, Johnnie Hamp.

The TV audiences loved *The Comedians*. They couldn't get enough of the quick-fire humour. Viewing figures were testimony to that fact. They were the cream of their profession. If they hadn't been, they would never have been able to keep up the standards for so long, which they undoubtedly did. So three years after the launch of the show, when it was at the height of its popularity, Johnnie Hamp turned once again to the working men's club theme for what turned out to be yet another massive hit – *The Wheeltappers and Shunters Club*.

This show, unlike *The Comedians* which featured close-ups of comics telling jokes, was played out on a broader canvas set in a club in the north of England, featuring the band under the direction of Derek Hilton, the turns – top international names mingled with virtually unknowns from the club circuit – and two key performers who had previously starred in *The Comedians* and had been brought up in working men's clubs themselves in Colin Crompton as club chairman and Bernard Manning as compere.

The Wheeltappers and Shunters Club, as *The Comedians* before it, was an instant hit with viewers.

Johnnie Hamp went on to bring many more spectacular shows to our screens and in so doing made big stars out of many performers who were relatively unknown nationally before making their television debut under his watchful eye and guidance.

But no matter how famous these performers became, they never forgot their roots.

I met one of them at a Press Ball at the Piccadilly Hotel in Manchester. After the television exposure he was in even bigger demand in clubs and summer season resorts. He was at the pinnacle of his career – and he was in plaster from hip to ankle.

What had he been doing? He had been doing two spots a night – an early one in Stoke on Trent and a later spot at a club several miles south of Birmingham.

He would do his first show, drive down to his second venue, do his second show, stay down there overnight, then drive back north to his home the next morning.

But on Christmas Eve he drove back north in the morning as usual, went down to Stoke and did his early evening show, then drove south to do his second show. But because it was Christmas, he wanted to get home. So instead of staying overnight, he decided to drive back.

He fell asleep at the wheel of his car, and woke up with it embedded in the bottom of a motorway bridge!

I asked him why he did it. He was a big name. He didn't have to race from one end of the country to the other like that.

The answer was simple. Old habits die hard. You never turn down work.

Colin Crompton's portrayal of the hapless club official got a lot of laughs, but a lot of his comedy wasn't far from the truth.

Concert secretaries really were a breed of their own.

I came across concert secretaries, who when asked what they were going to do about the Sex Discrimination Act would have said unhesitatingly: 'I've not seen them myself but if you think they're any good, book 'em.'

Comics had to perform before or after bingo sessions, support the latest singing sensation or specialist act, work between frames in a snooker final while the players had a break, or provide a spot of light relief during a darts match. Which was all hard graft, because the darts or snooker or bingo or musical turn were the main event of the evening, and the comic was just there to support.

The result was that despite their best efforts, there were times when they could have a real struggle on their hands to get even the slightest acknowledgement that they were in the same room, never mind get the undivided attention of their audience.

But perhaps one of the most bizarre experiences I heard about from a club comic was when he was booked to appear at a minor sporting club in the north of England. He hoped he had asked all the right questions to make sure that he was the big attraction, that he would have the undivided attention of his audience and he would not be going on at a time when they were about to take bookings for the forthcoming outing to Boddington's brewery.

He wasn't disappointed. He turned up to find he was certainly the star comic on the bill. He was the only one – everyone else was a boxer.

He had been booked to entertain during a break in the bouts and had to do his act from the middle of the ring!

But it was another club comic who faced not only one of the most difficult moments in his career, but probably in the career of any turn who ever performed in the northern clubs.

It happened while he was working at a club in north Manchester.

He had been on for about five minutes, long enough for the audience to realise there was an entertainer in their presence and for them to start to take notice, when he was interrupted in the middle of his act by the concert secretary coming on stage, taking the microphone off him, and solemnly announcing the tragic death in a road accident of the club treasurer.

He gave a brief resume of the life of the dear departed, recalled his lengthy connection with the club, his unswerving dedication and service to his fellow members over many years, expressed his consolations (sic) to his widow, then called for a minute's silence.

Then, with the members by now in a complete state of shock, he handed the microphone back to the comic and said: 'Carry on, lad!'

19

HOW CAN I MAKE THE WORLD LAUGH TODAY?

FOR MANY COMICS their work is a way of life. If they are not performing, they are constantly looking for new material. And if there is one person in front of them, they have an audience.

But not everyone would see the funny side.

I was leaving the Granada TV Centre with Bernard Manning one evening just before Christmas. As he passed the security man on reception, he wished him all the best and stuffed something into his top pocket, with the words 'Have a drink on me'.

The security man thanked him, wished him and his family a happy Christmas, and as we were leaving, took the offering from his pocket.

It was a tea bag!

During my years with *Coronation Street*, a number of actors with a variety background became regular members of the cast, and I'm proud to say good friends over the years. We would spend hours in the green room reminiscing about the golden years of variety, they happy to talk endlessly about their careers and the legends they had worked with, while I took such great delight in relishing every word, every anecdote.

I first met Amanda Barrie when I started work on *Hickory House*, a children's series which she co-presented with Alan Rothwell. Their co-stars were an animated mop head and a stuffed cushion, given a life of their own by puppet master Barry Smith.

Amanda's TV and film work could hardly have been more wide ranging. As a dancer she had appeared on the West End stage, and had worked in many TV shows with some of the biggest names in the business. She was one of the first Lionel Blair dancers, worked with Hughie Green on *Double Your Money* and joined the *Carry On* team for *Carry on Cabbie* and *Carry On Cleo*.

Amanda and I were to meet up again many years later when she appeared in *Coronation Street* as Alma Sedgwick to take over the running of the café, a role which spanned the entire range of emotions over the years as her character developed into one of the strongest in the cast.

If anyone justifies the title of show business all-rounder, Amanda certainly does.

I also had the great pleasure for many years of working with Alan, who has had such a distinguished career in radio television and the theatre, both as actor and director. Again there was a *Coronation Street* connection. In the early days he played David Barlow, younger brother of Ken, among his many and varied roles.

We worked together on many schools and pre-school programmes. I have the greatest admiration for his talent and professionalism. Whether he was presenting *Picture Box* to young viewers or performing *The Prophet* for a discerning adult audience, he always commanded their undivided attention. And above all, Avril and I have valued his friendship, and that of his family.

Betty Driver was another vastly experienced and accomplished performer when she arrived on the cobbled streets of Weatherfield, and a lady with whom I spent many an enjoyable moment reminiscing about the good old days of music hall during a break in rehearsals in the *Coronation Street* green room.

She had been encouraged by her mother to perform from being a child, and by the time she was 11 she had turned professional. After working in rep, she made her first London stage appearance at the age of 14 in a variety show at the Prince of Wales theatre. She was to go on to play in many revues and become a major recording artiste.

For seven years, she worked with Henry Hall and the BBC Dance Orchestra as well as appearing in a number of films. Her first contact with *Coronation Street* was when she auditioned for the role of Hilda Ogden.

Bill Tarmey, who played loveable rogue Jack Duckworth for so many years, came to the show from the club circuit. He spent his evenings singing in cabaret, working in the building trade during the day, but he eventually gave up his day job to take minor parts on television.

He never had an audition for Jack Duckworth. He'd been seen on screen in the programme for years as an extra throwing darts or downing a pint in the background. Eventually he was given the occasional line or two, and it just grew from there.

Liz Dawn, who played his long-suffering wife, Vera, came from a similar background. She, too, was a popular club performer. Her early acting roles were minor, too, as she worked the cabaret circuit in the evenings.

Her first appearance in *Coronation Street* was as a troublesome factory worker, which she played on and off for almost a decade, before becoming a permanent fixture, and with husband Jack, one of the most popular double acts in the history of the show.

Lynn Perry was another who came to the show from clubland. She had been working the cabaret circuit since the 1960s, supporting top acts from this country and further afield, including the Beatles in their heyday.

Lynn came from a showbiz family, Her brother is actor and comic Dougie Brown, one of the regulars on *The Comedians*.

Her first acting role was as the mother in the film version of *Kes*. *Coronation Street* director Paul Bernard had seen the film, remembered Lynn's performance when he was casting for Ivy Tilsley and she too became one half of another of the great double acts, with Peter Dudley playing husband Bert.

Both the Duckworths and the Tilsleys arrived in a way that was fairly typical of how families were built in *Coronation Street*. Vera and Ivy were both working in the factory, and after they became established as the strong characters they were, it was decided at story conference that it would be interesting to have a look at their families. So Jack and son Terry, played by Nigel Pivaro, and Bert and son Brian, played by Chris Quinten, were introduced in the hope that they would give us new story avenues to explore as the new characters developed.

And did they do that!

The Percy, Sam and Phyllis trio of 'golden oldies' was a huge hit with viewers, and they were pure gold to write for.

I have already mentioned the glittering career in variety of Bill Waddington. His *Corrie* character as tetchy Percy Sugden, the old soldier who 'made gravy under gunfire', was to bring him world wide fame after he had all but retired from the business.

Sam Tindall was played by Tom Mennard and Phyllis Pearce by Jill Summers, two more veterans of variety who finished their long and distinguished careers with character parts in *Coronation Street*.

Tom had a wonderful, dry sense of humour, and had been a firm favourite with theatre and radio audiences for many years. His weekly radio series, *Local Tales*, which recounted the adventures of Tom with his three pals, Charlie, Harry and Fred, were real gems.

Tom wasn't so much a teller of jokes – he was a genuinely funny man who tried to find humour in any situation.

I am convinced that he used to wake up every morning and think 'How can I make the world laugh today?'

The first time I was out socially with Tom was at a rather posh dinner for charity in a very upmarket hotel.

It was a black tie function, but Tom didn't possess a dinner suit. So he did what I later discovered was quite a regular occurrence with Tom when he wanted to wear something special – he went to the Granada TV wardrobe department.

Tom selected one from stock that he thought would be suitable for the occasion. It wasn't the smartest or most modern. In fact I think the last time it had seen the light of day was probably in *Lost Empires*.

But it suited Tom down to the ground – literally. Because apart from everything else about it, whoever it was made for originally, it was definitely not for a man of Tom's stature, but for someone at least three sizes bigger.

But he knew that it would get a laugh.

After the meal, he stood up and opened his speech by saying they'd had a sweep on what was in the soup – and the chef had come third!

It brought the house down, and very nearly the chef's meat cleaver into Tom's skull. But that was Tom Mennard, one of life's genuinely funny men who couldn't resist getting a laugh out of any situation.

One afternoon he turned up at the Victoria and Albert Hotel in Manchester, told the girl on reception that he had come for the kami kazi pilots' reunion and could she tell him if any of the others had arrived yet.

He told one of the check-out girls in his local supermarket

he'd just got a new microwave fireplace. It was a wonderful thing. You could spend a whole evening in front of it in just eight minutes.

He arrived at the studios one day with half his face painted white and told anyone who would listen that he was auditioning for *Phantom of the Opera*.

On another occasion he turned up swathed in black bin bags and told everyone that he had come to audition for *Batman*.

Jill Summers, another one of our wonderful characters steeped in the traditions of variety, was another great joker.

Jill played Phyllis Pearce, the third member of the infamous trio of Percy, Sam and Phyllis.

She had over 50 years experience in variety before she took on the role of Phyllis. She followed her parents into showbusiness. Her father was a tightrope walker in a circus and her mother was in revue.

She had initially appeared as a vocalist and during the war she had served with ENSA, entertaining troops who didn't always fully appreciate singers.

One day, she tripped as she made her entrance, came out with a mouthful of abuse that any squaddie would have been proud of and brought the house down. It launched her career as a comedy turn and she never looked back, and as I was to find out when out with her on many a social occasion, there was no way her colourful language had been diminished by the years!

She worked in many musical revues and had many TV roles before taking on the role of Phyllis.

One of the reasons the Percy, Sam and Phyllis relationship worked so well was that when the three characters were brought together to create that little bit of pure gold for the writers and for our *Coronation Street* viewers, not only were they totally convincing in their roles, but they knew each other so well, having previously worked together in variety, and they all had that wonderful sense of comic timing.

That is not to say that they could only play comedy or play off each other. They were accomplished performers and could just as easily adapt to more dramatic situations in any scenario with any other member of the cast, as they frequently did.

And they were another example of how our show was enriched by some of the finest pros from the variety circuit blending in with our wonderful team of actors to provide so many opportunities to the writers to come up with the stories to keep *Corrie* at the top of the ratings.

Jill, like Tom, was another one who never missed an opportunity to get a laugh.

One of her favourite party pieces was to go to the ladies loo at whatever function she happened to be attending, the posher the better, to return with the back of her dress tucked into the top of her ample knickers – and then enjoy the expressions on the faces of others, too embarrassed to mention it.

She got her final laugh at her own funeral. At the end of the service, after Roy Barraclough had delivered a warm tribute and folk were leaving the crematorium, their thoughts dominated by fond memories of a wonderful lady who had brought sunshine into the lives of so many, a hand appeared from between the closed curtains and waved!

20

A PREDICTION COMES TRUE

BY THE EARLY 1970s, many traditional variety theatres had been turned over to bingo, bowling alleys or gone dark because the cost of refurbishment of such old buildings was prohibitive. But different venues were springing up which were providing new opportunities for the big name variety acts who were benefiting from television exposure – cabaret clubs.

These glittering establishments had their roots in the working men's clubs, in as much as there was more informality and a more convivial atmosphere than in the traditional theatres, but the surroundings were opulent and the refreshment that was readily available was much more than a bag of crisps or a meat pie.

Instead of the run of the mill club act, the audiences were now treated to top class entertainers from both sides of the Atlantic in a comfortable, relaxed atmosphere where they could have a meal and a drink or two, all served at their table.

The era of the cabaret club had arrived.

The north of England was a hotbed of such clubs, some of them seating upwards of 1000 people. My local venue was the Golden Garter in Manchester, which was fairly typical of so many others that abounded at that time. Among them were The Talk of the North, Fagins, Bernard Manning's Embassy Club, Frank Lamar's Foo Foo's Palace, the Northern Sporting Club, Southern Sporting Club, Poco a Poco, The Willows to name but a few in the Manchester area, with just as big names on the other side of the Pennines, the Batley Variety Club being just one.

Darrell's club in Wythenshawe, previously a bowling alley, was reborn as the Golden Garter on Monday, 7th October 1968, when the top of the bill was Bruce Forsyth. A menu from November of that year boasted a three course meal, including steak if you wanted it, at a cost of 13s.6d or 67.5 pence in today's money. Top of the bill on that occasion was Eartha Kitt.

Bruce Forsyth and Eartha Kitt were two of the biggest names in entertainment from both sides of the Atlantic, and that standard was maintained for more than a decade as punters tucked into one of the gastronomic favourites of the day – prawn cocktail, followed by chicken in a basket, all washed down with a glass of sauternes – before the club's eventual demise.

So with these cabaret clubs at a peak of popularity in the 1970s, it is hardly surprising that there was a cross-over between acts from shows like *The Comedians* and *Wheeltappers and Shunters* Club and clubs like the Golden Garter.

And with the television exposure putting them firmly at the top of the popularity stakes, comedians and club acts who had been toiling around the working men's club circuit for years, finally had the chance to hit the big time.

Stan Boardman, Jim Bowen, Duggie Brown Frank Carson, Colin Crompton. Ken Goodwin, Bernard Manning, George Roper, Roy Walker, Charlie Williams, Mick Miller and many, many more who had been working the clubs for years and had become names that were familiar the length and breadth of the country through television, found themselves topping variety bills in theatres, glittering cabaret clubs and seaside shows nationwide.

And it wasn't just the comedians. There were speciality acts, vocalists, musicians. Shep's Banjo Boys became one of the most popular musical acts in the north of England, with non-stop demand for their distinctive brand of entertainment not only for variety shows, but corporate and private functions, and cruising too. All this as well as a residency at the Golden Garter.

Thanks in no small part to television and the exposure it brought, variety was experiencing yet another golden era.

The public's appetite for popular entertainment fuelled the search for new talent through television shows like *Opportunity Knocks* and *New Faces*, which launched another generation of variety stars into becoming top attractions, and in some cases, national treasures.

One of the earliest talent shows was *The Carroll Levis Discovery Show*, which gave unknown performers the chance of performing in front of a wider audience.

Carroll Levis, a Canadian by birth, moved to England in his mid-20s, and travelled the country hosting talent shows for young people. This was extended to radio when he joined the BBC in the early 1950s, and eventually to television. .

Opportunity Knocks was another touring talent show that was produced for radio in the early 1950s, before transferring to television with spectacular success. Hosted by Hughie Green, *Opportunity Knocks* was attracting regular audiences approaching 20 million at the peak of its popularity, and was responsible for launching the television careers of many, many star names.

Hughie Green's *Opportunity Knocks* ended in 1978, but it was revived almost a decade later hosted by Bob Monkhouse, and eventually by a former winner who had himself become a massive star, Les Dawson.

New Faces made its first appearance in the 1970s, hosted by Derek Hobson. But the show differed from *Opportunity Knocks* in its method of declaring a winner. It didn't depend on audience applause, but had a panel of judges.

But like *Opportunity Knocks*, it had the same effect on countless show business careers, giving a first public television airing to acts who were to go on to become show business legends. One such young lady from Sheffield was the much-missed Marti Caine, who went on to emulate Les Dawson, hosting the talent show that had first launched her into the ranks of the comedy greats. With the tragic passing of Marti, Les and so many other brilliant entertainers, we lost some of the brightest stars in the business.

The growing number of shows featuring members of the public who were more than willing to provide the entertainment, were soon joined by another television success story – the game show. And the format for the shows was almost as diverse as the contributions by those taking part.

Game for a Laugh, Blind Date, Stars in Your Eyes, Mr and Mrs, The Golden Shot, The Generation Game, 3-2-1, The Price is Right , Family Fortunes, Play Your Cards Right – the list and variety of shows went on and on.

And with the increasing number of reality shows and latterly quiz shows, the entertainment scene was moving yet again into a new era, giving more and more people from every walk of life the chance of fame and fortune.

THE WRITER'S TALE

21

WRITING? THAT'S NOT A JOB!

WHILE THE GREAT ITV revolution was taking place in the world of entertainment, writing for television was the last thing in my mind.

I was taking the first tentative steps along the path of my chosen profession. I was working in weekly newspapers as a reporter, feature writer, sports writer, sports editor, sub editor (in the case of one small weekly newspaper group, all at the same time!) in my progression towards becoming news editor then editor with a much respected group of weekly newspapers in Cheshire.

It was a path that was not unfamiliar to many of the writers of *Coronation Street* when I joined the team. Many of them had worked on newspapers, magazines, in advertising or public relations before moving to the challenging world of television. And it wasn't confined to *Coronation Street*.

Many newspaper journalists had formed the basis of the current affairs staff, programme presenters, reporters, researchers and producers in those early days of commercial television. Many, of course, went on to become legends in the world of television broadcasting as they rose to the new challenge, producing and working on some of the most innovative programming of the day. Others rapidly became household names in front of the cameras.

My career in journalism started out as a fairly low-key affair. The reason I was working as a reporter/feature writer/sports writer/sports editor/sub editor/compiler of births, marriages and deaths notices in alphabetical order and occasionally writing the *In Your Stars* column was that the entire editorial staff on my first newspaper, including the editor, numbered five – and two of those were part-timers. But it was a start.

Needless to say, the paper didn't have a massive circulation. I realised that when on the way to my interview I called in at a newsagent and asked if he had a copy.

He told me he had just sold it!

Working on a weekly newspaper in a Cheshire town in the 1960s was hardly the stuff of Hollywood movies.

A crime wave where I worked would have been someone edging through a halt sign without stopping, riding a bike on the pavement or leaving a car on the highway after dark without a parking light.

There was some excitement one day when a girl reported an incident of indecent exposure at a local beauty spot. It had happened one morning when she was walking her dog, and although she gave the police a description of sorts – big man, well built, dark hair – they never caught the offender. To be fair, they didn't have a lot to go on. The girl in question said she never saw his face.

My world rapidly became a matter of covering local events and council meetings.

But I was to spend many happy years at the heart of a very warm and close community, eventually becoming editor of the paper.

Being the editor of a local weekly newspaper in those days brought all sorts of riches – reserved seats at amateur dramatic society performances, guest of honour at harvest festivals, May Queen celebrations, even a spot in the annual Civic Parade, where my wife and I marched proudly in the procession behind the local brass band and the Councillors themselves, admittedly much nearer to the rear of the parade than the front.

Eventually the time came to move on to widen my horizons, and that moment came when an opportunity arose to join the features staff of the Daily Mirror in Manchester. The working week was four days, one of which was Sunday, and the hours were afternoons and evenings.

This was ideal, because by now I had started to write and sell one or two bits and pieces to radio and TV programmes – mainly sketches for comedy shows. But the biggest factor influencing my decision to give up the cosy lifestyle of editing a weekly newspaper was that I had already started to write for *Coronation Street*.

My new working pattern as a member of the Daily Mirror features staff gave me the chance to work more hours as a television and radio writer, to increase my output and to be available for meetings, conferences and rehearsals while still having the security of a paid job.

In those days, my hours of work, enjoyable as they may have been, were long – more so when I gave up my Saturday afternoons and evenings, too, to work on the sports desk of the Sunday Mirror.

It wasn't unusual to finish a *Coronation Street* story conference, or a rehearsal or recording day, or a day of read-throughs for a schools series I was writing, then to race over from the Granada Television studios in Manchester to the offices of the Mirror in Withy Grove to start the late shift in the features department at five o'clock – and on occasion, if a big story broke during the evening, that could last until three in the morning.

And that was the pattern of my life until I finally took the decision to commit fully to being a freelance writer. Even then I continued to edit the TV programme listings for the Mirror, which meant racing across the city at lunchtime between television studios and newspaper office to pick up the hand-outs and programme summaries from the broadcasting companies so I could take them home, work on them there, and return the edited version the following day.

But in spite of all this frenzied activity, brought about no doubt through observation of the first rule of being a freelance – or anyone in the entertainment business for that matter trying to establish themselves in their chosen profession – you never turn down the chance of work.

One of the first things I discovered about being a writer is the near-impossibility of convincing people that you actually do it for a living. That for the most part, it is an honest, decent, legal calling that occupies most of your waking hours.

Especially working for a show like *Coronation Street*.

When people first learned that I wrote for *Coronation Street*, they would still ask what I did for a living. These were, in the main, viewers who thought that the actors made it up as they went along. Which, I suppose, is as good an endorsement as you can get that you are doing a convincing job.

And I quickly discovered that no matter how committed you are, not everyone sees the way you earn a living in quite the same way as you do.

I was on holiday and trying to explain with as much pride as I could muster the intricacies and responsibilities of being a writer to a former miner-turned-pig farmer.

He had asked me what I did for a living during the normal course of our conversation, and I thought freelance writer may have been sufficient of an explanation.

He looked puzzled. So I tried to explain in more detail.

I told him at some length about the need to continually look for potential markets, research your subject, working with the written and spoken word. Your quest to inform, educate and entertain. How, before you put pen to paper, there was the need to ask those all important questions. Who was your audience? Were they young? Old? Was your work intended for press? Radio? Television? Would the treatment be drama? Comedy? Documentary?

He listened intently, his head inclined, gently drawing on his pipe. He didn't comment, but I knew, I just knew that I had eventually got through to him.

Here was a man of the world who was now savouring every word I said, understanding exactly where I was coming from. Who recognised the importance of my mission in life, the passion that drove my very existence.

I summed it all up by proudly explaining that my main aim in my work, whatever discipline I was working in, was to paint pictures in words. Vivid, colourful, action-packed, attractive pictures that would enhance the eye and mind of the beholder.

He was silent for some time as he reflected upon what I had said, before coming out with words I will never forget:

'That's not a job!'

And he wasn't the only one who looked at it like that. Many people would see my working life that way.

I could be working on three different television shows at the same time, editing the TV programme pages of the Daily Mirror, organising pictures for the sports pages for seven or more editions of the Sunday Mirror on a Saturday night, and people would still say: 'But what do you do for a job?'

There were times when it was easier not to even try to enlighten folk.

One occasion that comes to mind is towards the end of my time with the Daily Mirror, when I took a four-week sabbatical.

Now when the staff took sabbaticals, it wasn't unusual for journalists to go mountaineering in the Himalayas, exploring the Andes, doing some overland trek for charity or voluntary work in some forgotten outpost of what used to be the British Empire.

I don't think my street cred gained anything at all when I revealed that I was taking a children's show – a TV spin-off – into the theatre, and was about to spend the next month directing a cast of five – two of whom were an animated stuffed cushion and a mop head!

When I moved into television it was an abrupt change of direction in my career path. I didn't realise it at first, but for me it signalled the start of an era when as a freelance writer I would be working or on call 24 hours a day, seven days a week not only on *Coronation Street* but on any writing opportunity that came my way from situation comedy to children's programmes, from dramatised documentaries for radio on some of our most outstanding figures in history to Basil Brush.

Joining the *Coronation Street* team changed my life, as it has done for the many thousands of folk who have worked for the show in one capacity or another during its glittering history.

22

STATESIDE TO MERSEYSIDE

ONE THING THAT I quickly learned, working for *Coronation Street*, was the phenomenal impact of the soap opera, or as we preferred to call it, continuing drama series.

So where did the 'soap opera' come from?

Well, as you might expect, from America.

Soap opera has its origins in radio broadcasting in the United States going back to the 1930s, and the generic name came from the fact that the programmes, mainly aired in the afternoon and aimed at housewife audiences, were sponsored by manufacturers such as Procter and Gamble, Colgate-Palmolive and Lever Brothers.

The first recorded soap opera, *Guiding Light,* was launched on American radio in 1937 and transferred to television in 1952, where it ran for many years.

Britain's earliest soap opera, to use the established generic term, was a radio drama called *The Robinsons*. It ran from 1942 until 1948, and was based on the lives of a front-line British family during wartime.

It was originally created to be broadcast to the United States and Canada on the BBC North American Service to demonstrate the courage of the British people. The drama was unashamedly politically- motivated propaganda intended to get the Americans into the war.

While *The Robinsons* was still running, during the post-war rationing period another radio drama serial was created, which was rapidly to become compulsive listening to a whole new generation of listeners.

Dick Barton – Special Agent ran from 1946 until 1951. It was eventually pulled off because it was considered to be becoming a bad influence on young listeners.

It was the demand for a rural *Dick Barton* that led to the creation of *The Archers* by Geoffrey Webb and Edward J Mason, who were working on *Dick Barton* at the time.

A pilot series was made in 1950, and it worked well enough for a further series to be commissioned, the first episode of which went out on 1st January 1951.

The Archers has gone on, of course, to become the longest-running and most successful continuing drama serial in the history of radio.

When *The Robinsons* finished in 1948, *Mrs Dale's Diary,* a daily account of the life of a doctor's wife, her family and friends, was created to fill the void. It was first broadcast on the old Light Programme in June of that year.

In February 1962, the title was changed to *The Dales*, and the show continued to air until 1969 on the newly-formed Radio 2, when it replaced the Light Programme in 1967. The serial was then replaced by *Waggoners' Walk*, which ran until 1980.

What is generally acknowledged to be the first British television soap opera was not made primarily for adults, but for children.

The Appleyards was broadcast live by the BBC fortnightly in the children's television slot on Thursday afternoons and followed the fortunes of a suburban home counties family, mum, dad and their four children. The series ran for five years between 1952 – 57, with each episode having a running time of 20 minutes.

In 1954, the BBC screened its first television soap opera aimed at an adult audience, *The Grove Family,* also filling a time slot of some 20 minutes. The series featured the highs and lows of an extended lower middle class family living in a

London suburb – mum, dad, four children with ages ranging between eight and 20, and an elderly grandmother.

The Grove Family, which ran for some three years, is generally accepted as the first domestic soap opera to be screened in this country.

By the time *The Grove Family* finished in 1957, ITV were realising the potential of the soap opera concept and during that same year, just 12 months after the last of the ITV franchises had been awarded, Britain's first twice-weekly ITV serial hit our screens.

Emergency Ward 10 was an on-going drama about the highs and lows in the world of the staff and patients in a busy hospital, Oxbridge General.

Medical matters have proved to be a very rich seam of drama, and *Emergency Ward 10* was to be the forerunner of many, many more British-based hospital series, including, *Angels, General Hospital, The Royal, Casualty, Holby City* to name but a few.

The popularity of *Emergency Ward 10* firmly established the genre of the twice- weekly drama serial, and in December 1960 the first episode of *Coronation Street* hit our screens. Originally scheduled for 13 weeks, it was to go on to become the most popular television continuing drama series in the world, still going strong more than half a century later.

The BBC, too, were by now well aware of the popularity of twice-weekly drama serials, and in 1962 they came up with one featuring the lives of the staff working on a glossy magazine.

Compact ran until 1965, when *The Newcomers* was launched. It followed the fortunes of another London family as they adapted to life on a housing estate in East Anglia, and ran until 1969. *Market in Honey Lane* was launched by the BBC in 1967, but only survived for a couple of years.

In 1969, Yorkshire Television launched *Castle Haven*, a series set in a large Victorian seaside house converted into flats.

It lasted barely twelve months, but it was interesting for the many names who went on to stardom in other TV long-running series, among them Roy Barraclough, Jill Summers and Ernst Walder, who all went on to appear in *Coronation Street;* and Kathy Staff, who created Doris Luke in *Crossroads* and later the unforgettable temptress Nora Batty in *Last of the Summer Wine*. Kathy, too, appeared briefly in *Coronation Street*.

The soap bubble had really caught the imagination of the nation, and in 1972 ITV launched another rural daytime drama series set in Yorkshire, *Emmerdale Farm*. It was to move to its evening slot six years later, and is now just *Emmerdale*.

Round about the same time that *Emmerdale Farm* hit the screens, ATV were launching a drama series of their own set in a Midlands motel.

Crossroads was to run continuously until 1988, before closing its doors. There was an attempt by Carlton TV to revive the show in 2001 with four of the originals among the cast, but it never took off and in August 2002, the motel closed for business for the last time.

Meanwhile, over at the BBC, 1985 saw the launch of what was to be its most successful TV drama series ever.

To this day, *Eastenders* holds the record for the biggest audience of any British soap – 30.15 million at Christmas 1986, when Den served divorce papers on Angie.

Many continuing drama series have followed, with varying but never as spectacular a degree of success in terms of longevity, as *Coronation Street, Eastenders* and *Emmerdale*. Scottish Television launched *Take the High Road*, which ran for 20 years; many more have followed, including *Albion*

Market, Hollyoaks, Family Affairs, Night and Day. There was the short-lived BBC drama set in Spain, *Eldorado,* and perhaps most notably *The Bill,* which had its roots in the 1980s and continued at the top of its genre until 2010.

But the drama serial that was to redefine the genre in this country hit our screens in 1982, when Phil Redmond's Mersey Television launched *Brookside,* which was set on a small housing estate in Liverpool.

Brookside, with its gritty realism, was to break new ground and push the boundaries of popular serial drama further than any ongoing drama series had ever attempted before, and it launched a number of spin-offs during its 21 years on our screens.

Phil Redmond grew up in Liverpool and since embarking on a career as a writer and television executive has made a tremendous contribution not only to television and theatre, but also to the culture of his home town.

As well as *Brookside,* he has created many other successful TV series, including *Grange Hill* and *Hollyoaks.*

He has worked tirelessly to put his city to the forefront of culture and entertainment over the years, taking on the chair of a number of cultural institutions. In 1989 he was appointed Honorary Professor of Media Studies at Liverpool's John Moores University.

Phil Redmond's impressive influence and impact on the entertainment scene not only in his native Liverpool but much further afield was recognised in 2004 when he was awarded the CBE, and he was further honoured by his native city when in 2008 he was appointed Creative Director when Liverpool became the European Capital of Culture, an honour for the city that he had worked tirelessly to achieve.

Coronation Street, Eastenders, Emmerdale, may reign supreme today. But for how long?

The answer, of course, is in the hands of the viewers. As long as they keep watching, the production companies will meet the demand.

Because like it or not, serial drama today is more than entertainment. For many folk, it is a way of life.

23

TREADING THE COBBLES

CORONATION STREET CAME into my life big time early in 1971.

The show was at the peak of its popularity. It had over the previous decade become established as a nationwide phenomenon. It had become part of the very fabric of British entertainment, the stars had become screen icons. Not only had they reached out to touch the hearts of over 20 million viewers, they had became a part of their lives, their families – my own included.

Then one morning, I received a letter from someone who was not only to change the course of my life and shape my career over the next 27 years, but who was to become one of the best and most trusted friends I ever made in television – the late Harry Kershaw.

When I came out of the Royal Navy in 1957. Granada TV had been on air for some 12 months. At that stage in my life it wasn't even a speck on my horizon – but it was for Harry Kershaw.

Harry's passion for writing, producing and directing had been centred around the activities of the Cheadle Hulme Players Amateur Dramatic Society, a group of considerably high standard and much revered in his home village in Cheshire. During the day, he worked in the insurance business.

He took up the new and exciting challenge of contributing scripts to Granada Television shortly after the company went on air in 1956, and by the end of 1960, when *Coronation*

Street hit the screen, he already had a number of high profile drama credits to his name.

Harry became the first script editor on *Coronation Street*, and when he penned episode 13 he became the first person other than creator Tony Warren to write for the show.

Over the next three decades until his retirement in 1988, he became one of the most important contributors to the show's success, a master of his craft and an enormous influence not only on the success of *Coronation Street* and a number of other shows he worked on, but also on the many, many folk who were fortunate enough to have worked with him – myself included.

There are countless writers who were given their chance to forge a long and successful career in television thanks to the encouragement of Harry Kershaw. He was a true professional in every sense of the word, who, at times in the most trying of circumstances, somehow always managed to keep his sense of humour and consideration for everyone he came into contact with.

During his television career, Harry's output was phenomenal. He contributed some 300 scripts to *Coronation Street* alone, had four spells as producer, was Executive Producer for seven years as well as writing scripts for many other series, a number of which he created himself. He wrote three novelisations based on *Coronation Street*, and published his own autobiography *The Street Where I Live* in 1981.

Harry Kershaw will go down in television history as making one of the most outstanding contributions to popular entertainment of the 20th century.

When I first met Harry, I was still working as a journalist, but I had already started to spread my wings into TV and radio writing. Inevitably, my sights turned to the most successful TV drama serial in the history of television, which happened to be produced just down the road from where I lived.

I had sent in a sample of my work some months before to then producer Jack Rosenthal.

Before putting pen to paper, I had diligently watched a number of episodes with a critical eye. I noted how many cast members there were in each episode, how many scenes, how many sets were used, how many exterior shots. I studied the characters, their relationship with each other, their speech patterns.

I noted that they didn't cut from an actor in one scene to the same actor in the next. If you wanted to feature a character in successive scenes, they walked out of one and into the next one. I also noted that there appeared to be three main story strands running through each episode.

Armed with this information, I turned my hand to a trial script, basing my work on a surmised continuation of the situations I had seen most recently on screen.

It was never intended that my effort would be considered for transmission. I knew the programme was planned way in advance, and by the time my script landed in the producer's office, the team would be several weeks along the line in forward planning terms.

But I hoped that the fruits of my labours would show that I had a feel for the programme.

When I received an acknowledgment, telling me that the producer had read my script with interest, had a full writing team at the moment, but would be in touch if the situation changed, it was more or less what I expected.

I thought nothing more of it, other than to make a mental note to perhaps try again in another six months or so.

Then some time after, the letter from Harry arrived.

He had taken over as producer of the show again, had read my script, which was still in a filing cabinet in the office, and he wondered if I may be interested in calling in for a chat.

Would I? I practically burned a hole in the carpet in my eagerness to get to the phone!

After attending a number of meetings, a couple of story conferences which dealt with the future planning of the show, and writing some trial scenes, Harry eventually gave me a full episode to write. After some fine tuning under his watchful eye, it was put into production.

Some six weeks after I had written my first script for *Coronation Street*, Harry gave me another episode to write, and told me that after I had written it, he would let me know whether or not he would be keeping me on the team.

I wrote the episode, it went into production, and he never did let me know whether he would be keeping me on or not.

But I was still there nearly 30 years later!

When I first joined *Coronation Street* some 10 years after the first episode was screened, the show had an audience of about 18 million.

This regularly went over 20 million when we had a big story, and peaked at over 26 million – almost half the population!

Granted in those days there was only BBC 1, BBC2 and ITV, so viewers had much less choice than they have today.

Right from the outset I knew I was joining a British institution – but I didn't realise just how much a part of people's lives it was. The viewers had really taken the show and its characters to their hearts.

Coronation Street was at the peak of its popularity because quite simply it had become a part of the British way of life.

And by December 2010, it had achieved the remarkable feat of having been a part of our lives for 50 golden years.

24

THE EARLY YEARS

WHEN CORONATION STREET was first transmitted at seven o'clock on the 9 December 1960, it went out live.

Immediately afterwards, the second show was recorded, which was to be transmitted a couple of nights later.

To give some idea of the skill of those pioneer actors, directors, writers – the entire production team – I should like to point out that an ITV half hour was 24 minutes 35 seconds. No more, no less.

This was to accommodate the commercials at either end and in the middle.

And the timing had to be spot on, because while the programme was screened from a central transmission point, the commercials were fed in up and down the country from their regional bases.

Not only did the actors have to give convincing live performances, but they had to do it to the second.

For that first episode of *Coronation Street*, there were a dozen or so roles created. Some major roles came out of suggestions from the show's creator, Tony Warren. All were auditioned for in the traditional way.

And for some members of that original cast, it provided a whole new career at an age when most folk were thinking of retirement.

Jack Howarth, who played Albert Tatlock, was 64 when he joined the cast. He had been in show business most of his life. His father had been a comic and Jack had been at school with Gracie Fields. He had spent many years touring with rep.

During the war, he had run a show in Colwyn Bay, North Wales.

He came to *Coronation Street* from another drama series, having played Mr Maggs in *Mrs Dale's Diary* on radio for 14 years.

He found he had another link from the past with the show when he met up again with William Roache. Jack's son, John, had been at boarding school with Bill.

Doris Speed, who played Annie Walker, was 61 when she joined *Coronation Street*. Her parents had been music hall artistes, and she had appeared in their act when she was just a toddler. But acting was not initially to be her main occupation.

At 14 she took a shorthand typing course, worked as a secretary and in her spare time acted in amateur dramatics, before spending many years in rep. She also did radio work in Manchester for the BBC, where she first met Tony Warren in a *Children's Hour* play. She obviously made an impression, because Tony remembered Doris when casting for his new twice-weekly drama series was underway, and she found a whole new career opening up for her.

Certainly she couldn't have dreamed that her new-found fame as Annie Walker would project her into one of the nation's favourite characters. Ironically, when the call came to join *Coronation Street* as the wife of the landlord of the Rovers Return, she was actually working for a brewery!

Arthur Lesley, who played her television husband Jack, was also from a showbiz family, and he too had spent a lifetime in rep before joining Doris as mine host of what was to rapidly become the most famous pub in the land.

Bernard Youens, who was to play Stan Ogden for the rest

of his working life, started his career in rep, his introduction to appearing in front of the cameras coming with Mancunian Films. But his career was interrupted for six years during the Second World War, when he served in North Africa, Anzio and Egypt. After the war, he returned to rep and originally auditioned for the role of Jack Walker. When he didn't get it, he was offered a job with Granada Television as a continuity announcer, which he held until he landed the role of Stan.

There were nearly 600 auditions for that first show, one of the hopefuls being William Roache, *Corrie*'s longest serving actor.

When he left boarding school, Bill was set to follow his father into the medical profession, but he joined the Army and became a regular officer in the Royal Welsh Fusiliers.

He decided to become an actor after leaving the Army, and after three years in rep, with four films and some TV work to his credit, the call came from *Coronation Street*.

In his character of Ken Barlow, he has had a relationship with almost every eligible girl who has walked the famous cobbles, and altogether had a far more eventful and interesting time of it than any other resident of a terraced street in the North of England could ever have dreamed of.

Perhaps his closest rival in the romance stakes was Mike Baldwin, played for over 30 years by Johnny Briggs. He may not have been there from day one, but he still managed to notch up 23 girlfriends, four wives and three children – that we know of!

Johnny had embarked on his showbusiness career at the age of 12, when he won a scholarship to the Italia Conte Stage School. His first stage engagement was as a boy soprano, but when his voice broke he went into rep. After National Service, he appeared in a number of TV shows, including *The Young Generation, Z Cars* and *The Avengers*.

He landed the role of Sergeant Russell in the long-running series *No Hiding Place*, and was one of the few faces well-known to TV viewers some time before *Coronation Street*.

When *Coronation Street* was initially cast, there was a general policy of going for actors virtually unknown to television audiences. This was so that they would be instantly believable as the characters they portrayed rather than be seen as the actors themselves. But right from the beginning, there was one major exception.

Violet Carson was one of the best known voices in the country. She had first been heard on air as a singer in 1935, her repertoire ranging from popular music to opera, with local dialect songs thrown in.

During the war she travelled the country entertaining troops. She went on to join *Children's Hour* on radio as Aunty Vi, where she would sing, tell a story, act in a play, or play the piano. And she became known to a much wider audience when she joined Wilfred Pickles as Violet on the piano in *Have a Go*.

She had first met Tony Warren when she was working at the BBC and he was a young actor in *Children's Hour.*

Many of those actors from the early days were new faces to television and went on very quickly to become national treasures. But as well as the principal characters, there were many who came into the show fleetingly before moving on to find fame and fortune in other areas of show business.

Among them was Davy Jones, who appeared briefly as Ena Sharples' grandson before going on to achieve world-wide fame as a founder member of *The Monkees*.

Richard Beckinsale, who also had a brief encounter with Ena when he played a police constable who arrested her, went on to become one of our finest and most popular comedy performers through such shows as *The Lovers, Porridge* and *Rising Damp*, before his sudden untimely death at the age of 30.

Pete Noone played Len Fairclough's son Stanley before becoming a pop idol as Herman of *Herman's Hermits* fame.

While Bill Kenwright, who played Gordon Clegg, moved on to become one of the most successful impresarios in the business, while indulging his passion for football through his role as chairman of Everton FC.

And I remember watching a rehearsal in which the course of true love between a young Kevin Webster and his then girlfriend didn't run smoothly, thanks to her involvement with another young man.

As I watched the trio at rehearsals with casting director Judi Hayfield, she whispered to me 'This boy is going to be big one day. Very big.'

Judi, as always, was an excellent judge of talent.

It was Michael Ball!

25

DOES THE SHOW REFLECT REAL LIFE? TO OUR VIEWERS, IT *IS* REAL LIFE

THERE WAS NO doubt at all that, to the majority of our audience, the characters who appeared on screen in *Coronation Street,* were real – an extension to their own families and circle of friends.

And the actors and actresses were not expected to do anything that would destroy this illusion.

If one of the girls wanted to change her hairstyle, or an actor wanted to grow a beard, they had to talk to the producer first to see if it could be written into the show, and more to the point, if it fitted the character.

What the actor wanted was not the main criteria. If it wasn't felt that any change would sit easily on the character, there was no way it would happen

In those early days, they weren't even permitted to do theatre or pantomime.

It was still to do with preserving the feel that the characters in *Corrie* were real, and if they were seen to have a life outside, it would threaten that belief. There was the odd member of the cast who would try to bend the rules, but the majority were happy to comply. They didn't carry it quite as far as seeking permission before they caught a cold, but some did take it more seriously than others.

I well remember one contracted young actress appearing at the door of the *Coronation Street* office one day after she had found out that she was expecting her first baby. The girl had come to see producer John Temple because she wanted to let him know in good time so that there could be some mention in future scripts to explain her changing shape.

It wasn't a good moment. John and I were working against the clock sorting out a script problem that had come up due to the sudden illness of one of our actors. It meant a rapid adjustment of some of the scenes in studio that week. If the girl was expecting hearty congratulations and a champagne celebration, she was disappointed.

John gave her a warm smile, told her that he was very pleased for her and politely asked when it was due. She told him some six months hence. Ever the diplomat, he thanked her for her concern for the show, and told her that they would discuss it at some other time, unless it came early – like in the next couple of hours!

John was producer of *Corrie* for some three years from 1985, though he was no stranger to the show. When I had first joined the team some 14 years before, John had been a storyline writer, together with Esther Rose and Harry Driver.

He was to go on to make a big contribution to Granada TV's comedy output, producing many sitcoms, including *The Glamour Girls, Foxy Lady, Take My Wife* and *The Cuckoo Waltz*.

After leaving *Coronation Street*, he went on to produce *Take the High Road* for Scottish Television and returned to his beloved comedy when he moved to Southern Television as Head of Light Entertainment.

Coronation Street was being watched regularly by over 20 million viewers in the UK – almost a third of the population at its peak. It was being seen in over 20 countries throughout the world.

Which makes you wonder how some of them coped with translation.

When you consider that 'out of sight, out of mind' may translate literally in some countries as 'invisible idiot'; that 'the spirit is willing but the flesh is weak,' may translate as 'the vodka is good but the meat is bad'; and 'ladies and gentlemen' may translate as 'water closets and urinals' – it does make you wonder what they would make of Hilda Ogden saying to Stan: 'Shift yourself, you great fat lummox, and mash the tea!'

So what makes *Coronation Street* so durable? It is a far different show today than it was in Episode One all those years ago. The show has certainly changed with the times to keep abreast of changing attitudes and the changing social scene. The technology has changed, as have the characters and many of the sets. The new set at Media City in Salford is amazing and a world away from when it all first started.

But the production values most certainly haven't. They are as strong today as they were in that very first episode.

Above all, the show continues to entertain each time an episode is transmitted.

The reaction of the viewers has always been phenomenal, and was a real eye-opener to me from the moment I joined the show.

Births, marriages, deaths, anniversaries, personal likes, dislikes, they all have to be strictly adhered to.

If we were to move the date of a character's birthday because we wanted to play it as a special occasion to fit in with our Monday, Wednesday or Friday transmission times, we would certainly know about it – from the hundreds of people who shared the same birthday!

I should like to mention at this point the invaluable contribution made to the show by our first historian, the late Eric Rosser. Eric had worked in the tax office. He had watched the first episode of *Coronation Street* while he was in hospital after two serious accidents.

As an interest, he started to keep files of data on each character as references came up on the screen. Every incident, important date, birthday, like, dislike, he catalogued. It was Eric's work that formed the basis of the writers' 'bible', a document that became increasingly lengthy as the show progressed, and his presence at story conferences with his unparalleled knowledge of the characters' background sparked many a new story strand in the show.

The role of archivist was eventually taken over by Daran Little, who not only continued with Eric's good work, but also became a valuable contributor to the show in many other ways, writing many books and eventually joining the team of writers.

The majority of our viewers weren't just eavesdropping on this parallel world that existed inside a box in the corner of their living rooms, they were part of it. It was the same as the relationship between the rep theatre audience and the company of actors. They belonged to each other, inhabited each other's world.

Our viewers would regularly write to the producer of the show about their own experiences and offer story material, often volunteering to play the role themselves if it involved a new character and they felt they would be suited to the part.

They applied for all manner of jobs when they became vacant – milkman, shop assistant, garage mechanic, bar staff. They were quite serious and often well qualified to fill the position they'd applied for.

Viewers would offer accommodation to any of our characters threatened with losing their home, either temporarily or permanently. They offered jobs to those out of work, about to lose their jobs or just looking for a change.

They would offer to help pay off debts or replace money, if any of our characters lost anything.

When anyone was in trouble, there was never any shortage of practical advice – from solicitors, bank managers, even the Citizens' Advice Bureau.

Whenever a house or business on the Street came up for sale, it was never a question of if but when a viewer or two would come in with an offer.

One lady who lost her window cleaner wrote in to ask if Stan Ogden would include her in his round.

Viewers tried to book their car in for servicing at the garage. They wanted to book the Rovers for functions – something they were able to do for a while, when the Granada Studios Tour opened to the public, and a replica Rovers Return was built as part of the attractions.

They wanted their papers delivered by the Kabin.

In one episode, a freezer in the Corner Shop appeared to have broken down. It hadn't. It had been unplugged as part of the storyline. But at the end of the episode, the viewers didn't know that. On the morning following transmission, a new freezer was delivered to Granada Television studios – a gift from a supplier who was also an avid fan!

Viewers would send cards for birthdays, marriages and anniversaries. They would send sympathy cards and flowers for funerals. The flowers, incidentally, as well as other gifts sent to our characters by well-meaning viewers mainly for special occasions, were passed on to local hospitals and retirement homes, who were pleased to have them. The patients were even more delighted when they knew they had come from *Coronation Street*.

And the girls sent in ear rings for Bet Lynch by the bucketful.

One little six-year-old sent Bet a treasured pair from her

dressing-up box at a time when our voluptuous barmaid was going through a lull in her romantic life, explaining that the ear rings had never failed to get the little girl a boyfriend!

When the Street's old folk were trying to raise money to buy a piano for the community centre, a number of concerned viewers rang up offering theirs.

Women viewers would write in to ask where they could get patterns for sweaters and jumpers worn by the cast.

They would want to know where they could get wallpaper, furniture or ornaments they had spotted in one of the sets, and felt that they would fit in perfectly in their own homes.

When Bert and Ivy Tilsley were decorating their front room, one viewer wrote in to point out that he had decorated his front room with the same wallpaper as the Tilsleys – only Bert had put his on upside down!

Another woman viewer had been to a Christmas Ball, and afterwards wrote in to the show to ask if we could change the curtains in the Rovers. Someone had pointed out to her that her expensive dress was of a very similar pattern.

Pensioners groups wrote to protest if our senior citizens seemed to have too much money to spend, they were too well dressed, or their hair looked expensively coiffured. Albert Tatlock came in for particular attention because he was always drinking rum.

It was explained that he only drank rum when he could get someone else to buy it, which was more or less every time he went into the Rovers.

Being so much under public scrutiny, we had to do all we could not to make mistakes – and if we did, to have a ready answer.

One viewer pointed out that we had an out of date boxing poster on the wall in the Rovers. It had been there for months.

We explained that it was still up because one of the lads on the bill was a local boy who had made good.

I was frequently asked why no one in *Coronation Street* seemed to go to the doctors. I explained that they did, but more often than not they would go on a Tuesday, Thursday or Saturday morning. Our show went out on Mondays, Wednesdays and Fridays, that's why the viewers hadn't noticed them going!

If we did occasionally make a slip that I couldn't readily explain, I couldn't think of anything better than Harry Kershaw's response.

He said we had two kinds of viewer – those who watched the show for entertainment and those who tried to spot mistakes.

We tried to cater for everyone!

26

EXTENDED FAMILIES

OUTSIDE THE STUDIOS, viewers would greet the actors as if they were the character they were playing, which was not surprising since they came into their homes three times a week. The show was so steeped in realism and the public's belief in the characters so unshakeable that they became a part of their very existence.

The actors in *Coronation Street* couldn't hang up their characters in their dressing rooms when the television recording was finished and resume normal lives. When they left the television studios, they were still the characters they played as far as the public were concerned. Wherever they went, they were looked on by the viewers as an extension to their own families.

One actor turned up in a hotel to be greeted warmly by the reception staff as the character he played. They recognised him immediately, announced excitedly to anyone within earshot that they had a celebrity in their midst, and kept him there until he signed autographs for everyone.

When he came to leave the following morning, he took out his cheque book to pay – only to be told that it was company policy not to accept cheques without some form of identification!

Another actor, who was playing a character working in the builder's yard in *Coronation Street*, was out with his wife for a meal when a lady, who was also waiting to have her order taken, overheard him ordering lobster.

She got up from her table, walked straight over to him,

accused him of betraying his working class and said she would never watch the programme again. With that she stormed out of the restaurant.

It wasn't uncommon for members of the public to be over familiar with members of the cast when they were out socially. They felt that they knew them that well. The actor could be having a quiet meal with his wife, when they would be spotted by a member of the public. The star struck fan would quite often just say 'Hello' or ask for an autograph. But for some, that wasn't enough. They would pull up chairs, call their companions over and attempt to join the actor and his wife at their table.

The ecstatic fan meant no harm. In fact the time to worry would have been if the actor had been totally unrecognised and ignored, But there were times when the cast did want privacy. It was a tricky situation and needed careful handling. The actor would do nothing to enhance his public persona if he told his fans that he didn't really want their company, no matter how tactful he was.

But one actor had what I thought was a brilliant way of dealing with the situation without causing offence.

He said how delighted he was to meet the person, and they were obviously keen fans of *Coronation Street*.

Not only was he pleased to talk to them, sign an autograph, or pose for a picture, he would be happy to have them join his table, if they could answer him one *Corrie*-related question. If not, perhaps they would go back to their own table and allow he and his wife to get on with their meal alone.

The fan would eagerly agree. They knew everything, when it came to *Coronation Street*.

With which the actor would ask them: 'What is the name of Minnie Caldwell's cat?'

Back came the reply without hesitation: 'Bobbie.'

'Ahh,' said the actor. 'That's his stage name.'

While the actors had got used to a degree of recognition during their days in rep or variety, in television it was a vastly different experience.

Wherever they went, they would be instantly recognised whether it was at a bar, a football match or in a restaurant. It needed a very strong personality to keep his or her feet on the ground, as all the pressures steered them away from those close to them. Away from their families and friends and increasingly towards the people who thought they were part of their lives now – the viewers.

They would greet the actors warmly, smile at them, put them on a pedestal so high they were almost in orbit.

There were some members of our cast who did manage to maintain their privacy. To completely separate their on screen character from their personal lives. But for many, while the attention they received as a result of their fame may have come initially as an intrusion, the feeling soon faded. If the public were so convinced by their performance that they saw the characters as real people, who were they to object? It was the ultimate accolade. They were successful in their jobs, their chosen profession.

And what's more, it was keeping them in a job!

As *Coronation Street* moved on, there was some easing in the restrictions allowing the stars of the show to take time out to do the occasional play in the theatre, or pantomime. But if they thought they would be going back to what they knew before TV stardom, they were mistaken.

The public's concept of them had changed. It was practically impossible to get the audience to believe that they were watching Pat Phoenix or Peter Adamson playing a character in whatever production they were in.

They were watching Elsie Tanner or Len Fairclough being somebody else.

Many of the older members of the cast used to tell me that the first real awareness of just how big a success the show had become was when they received the ultimate accolade of the day – being invited to switch on Blackpool illuminations.

They drove from St Anne's to Blackpool Town Hall in an open-topped bus, and the route was lined from start to finish on both sides with masses of people, all eager for a glimpse of their idols.

As one actor told me, who was present on that occasion and was completely overwhelmed by the public response: 'I don't think any of us fully realised until that moment that what we were doing was manufacturing pure magic.'

There was, however, at least one person who was completely unmoved by the aura surrounding *Coronation Street* – and he worked within a stone's throw of the Granada Television studios in Manchester where the show was produced.

The story being played out was centred on a fishing trip, and for the filming the director and production manager had chosen a location along a stretch of the Manchester Ship Canal.

So on one gloomy, drizzly morning, a Granada film crew arrived on the banks of the canal at eight o'clock to film the scene, featuring Len Fairclough, Stan Ogden and Charlie Moffitt.

It was barely light, as the three actors – Peter Adamson, Bernard Youens and Gordon Rollings – sat there, cold and wet, while the director worked out his shots with the production manager and the camera, sound equipment and lighting were set up.

The actors were each handed a rod and proceeded to 'fish' the swirling, murky waters, as the camera rolled. They had hardly had time to exchange the opening lines of the scene, when further along the canal bank a slight, agitated figure appeared shuffling towards them pushing his bike, unbuttoned oversize raincoat flapping around the lower regions of his legs.

He completely ignored the camera, the sound engineer and the lights, walked straight into the middle of the scene and proclaimed with as much authority as he could muster: 'You can't fish here'.

While the director was hopping about as if on hot coals, the production manager tried to explain that they weren't actually fishing, and that they would have thought that the lights, cameras and sound equipment may just have given the interloper a slight hint that they were in fact filming.

The interloper was completely undeterred. 'It's fellers like you that make my job so difficult, you know. Now I'm telling you. You can't fish here. Not unless you've got a permit.'

And in spite of everyone doing their utmost to try to convince him that they weren't fishing, he was having none of it. He resolutely stood his ground.

Eventually, and in the interests of breaking the impasse, the production manager asked where a permit may be obtained.

The little man triumphantly produced a soggy booklet from his pocket, solemnly asked for the names of the three actors, wrote them down on three slips of paper and pocketed the three shillings fee, explaining forcibly that the permits would expire at sunset.

As he started to walk away, he glanced back at them, shook his head and said: 'You'll not catch anything here.'

And with that, he moved off and disappeared into the ever-thickening blanket of drizzle.

Not once did he show the faintest glimmer of recognition of three of the best-known faces on television at the time.

Despite the popularity of *Coronation Street* and all the fame and adulation it had brought to its stars, there was at least one man who had apparently never heard of Len Fairclough, Stan Ogden and Charlie Moffitt – or if he had, he couldn't care less.

They were intruding on his territory without a permit – and that was that!

27

WORKING AWAY? OH NO HE ISN'T!

THE SHOW WAS so true to life that viewers frequently confused the fiction with reality.

We ran a big story over a number of weeks where a character called Alan Bradley swindled Rita Fairclough out of a lot of money, and was trying to track her down with murderous intent. Rita fled to Blackpool, with Bet, where they booked into a hotel.

During the first part of the episode as the tension built, we cut between scenes of Rita and Bet in Blackpool and Alan in Weatherfield, desperately trying to find out where Rita was.

Then just before the advertising break Alec Gilroy inadvertently let slip to Alan in the Rovers bar where Bet and Rita were staying.

In the scripts, we had given the girls' hotel a fictitious name – which isn't easy in Blackpool. Almost anything you can think of, you can almost guarantee that there is a hotel or boarding house of that name.

During one scene close to the advertising break in part one, Bet and Rita were seen entering the hotel and for no more than a split second the nameplate revealing the real name of the hotel was on screen.

But it was long enough for our eagle-eyed viewers.

During the advertising break, the hotel switchboard was jammed as viewers rang to tell Rita that Alan was on his way!

Alan Bradley met his end when he was hit by a tram on Blackpool promenade. Our sharp-eyed viewers noted the number, of course. And for weeks after, the driver of that numbered tram, whether it was the same tram or the same driver or not, was hailed as a celebrity by holidaymakers who were queuing up for his autograph!

As a sequel to that particular story, I took a call in the *Coronation Street* office one lunchtime from a lady who asked to speak to Rita.

Unless the caller was known to us, if we couldn't deal with them there and then, the usual procedure was to say that we would tell the actor or actress that we had taken the call and hopefully they would call back.

Now if anyone asked for one of our cast members by the name of the character, it obviously wasn't a personal call. So in this case, I told the caller that if she would tell me what she wanted, I would make sure the actress got the message.

The caller, who was in a state of some excitement, told me it was very urgent. Could I tell Rita that Alan Bradley wasn't dead.

She'd just seen him in a department store in Manchester buying a shirt!

In another storyline in the show, we had one character who was put in secure accommodation after attacking Emily Bishop with a knife.

Two weeks after the episode where he was taken away was transmitted, the actor was opening a summer fair at a local hospice.

As he performed the opening, one lady was overheard saying to her companion 'Isn't it good of them to let him out to open the fair today.'

If one of our regulars wanted time out of the show for a holiday or for some other reason, we would usually do one of two things.

We would either just not see them or we may give a reason on screen for their not being there.

But there was no fooling some of our viewers!

Peter Dudley, who played Bert Tilsley, was on holiday for a couple of weeks. As the Tilsley family were fairly heavily involved in almost every episode at the time, to explain his absence, on screen we had packed him off to visit a desperately sick relative in Huddersfield.

One keen viewer rang in to tell us that he had been lying about the sick relative. She had been shocked to see him going into a holiday cottage in Devon – and with another woman! Would we please tell Ivy that he had been lying, but break it to her as gently as possible. She knew how much she was devoted to Bert.

What we didn't tell the viewer was that if she had looked a bit more closely at Peter's companion, she would have had an even bigger shock. It was Pat Phoenix!

Geoff Hughes, who was playing loveable rogue Eddie Yeats, had a story that took him away from *Coronation Street* for a few weeks. He had supposedly gone to help out an old pal with a big job he had on.

It wasn't long before we had a call from a viewer to tell us that Eddie had fabricated the whole story about going off to help out a mate.

He was actually in pantomime in Sunderland!

We ran one dramatic story which saw Elsie Tanner running away to London. No one in the Street knew where she was, and the whole episode was played around the anxiety of everyone back home wondering what could have happened to her.

At the end of the episode, we saw her knocked down by a taxi.

Within minutes, the Granada switchboard was jammed with viewers ringing up to tell her husband where she was and what had happened to her!

It was one more example of how the work of the whole team came together to provide such convincing characters and storylines that they were totally believed by the viewers.

28

OUT OF SIGHT – BUT NOT OUT OF MIND

FOR THE MOST part, viewers were only too ready to believe that the characters were around, even if they didn't see them.

One of our major stories, involving a character who had been a lynchpin of the series for many years, was the dramatic on-screen death and funeral of Len Fairclough.

A friend of mine said to me we were going to miss him. His character had been a corner stone of the street for so long. His romantic entanglements with Elsie Tanner were legend and had given us some of the most dramatic and gritty moments in the show.

I asked my friend how long he thought it was since he had last seen Len Fairclough on screen. He thought it was probably a couple of weeks.

In fact, it was months. And it was one more example of keeping the 'presence' of a character very much alive, even though they weren't physically there.

I took a call in the office one day from one lady who said she was very glad to see that Annie Walker was back and would I give her the caller's best wishes. The actress had been written out for a while due to a real-life illness, which everyone knew about as it was in the papers. We hadn't given a reason for her on-screen absence. We just didn't see her. But I wasn't too sure where the viewer was coming from as the actress, Doris Speed, was not yet back at work.

I said I would be pleased to pass on the caller's best wishes, but, tried to explain, the actress wasn't back yet.

But the viewer insisted she was. She distinctly heard Bet on screen the night before say she was going into the back to have a word with Mrs Walker!

And the viewers' concern for our characters wasn't restricted to those they had seen on screen.

One venture I became involved with was a telephone chat line.

Viewers could ring a number and hear the voice of a different one of our characters each week up-dating the story situation as seen on screen and chatting generally about aspects of street life and local folk, many of whom had never appeared in the show.

It was a labour of love to me. Each week I would select a character, write my brief piece, and the actor or actress and I would stay on after the week's technical run to do the sound recording.

One day a get-well card for a Mrs Giddings appeared in the office. It was a character that no one had ever heard of, so I had a phone call from the producer's secretary asking if I could throw any light on the mystery. After some thought I remembered that on that week's chat line, Mavis had mentioned having called in to see a Mrs Giddings, one of their customers, who was recovering from a major operation, and she was pleased to say she was making good progress towards a full recovery!

And it wasn't just viewers who could be confused between what went on in their own lives and what they had seen on TV. Even the most seasoned of us could go down that road.

I clearly remember one occasion when I was at an awards lunch at the Grosvenor House Hotel in London with Harry Kershaw.

We were chatting at the pre-lunch drinks reception, when Harry looked over my shoulder.

'That man behind you. I know him from somewhere. Isn't it Roy from the joiner's shop?'

I glanced behind me then turned back to face Harry.

'No, Harry. That's Ernie Wise.'

A few minutes later, his attention was taken by an adjacent female chatting animatedly to her companion.

'I know that face,' he said. 'Don't tell me. It'll come in a minute.'

After a brief pause, his face lit up as recognition dawned.

'Edna. From wardrobe.'

Again I had to correct him.

'No Harry. That's Esther Rantzen.'

Viewers would regularly write in with story ideas, but they were rarely used. Not always because they were totally unsuitable, but because many of them were sparked by what was being played out on screen at the time.

As we planned our storylines some three months ahead of transmission, in our forward planning we were well past what was being seen on screen.

The writers and the production team are always extremely careful and thorough with research, and we have always gone to great lengths to ensure authenticity. That could mean anything from spending hours in a mail order warehouse or overnight in a special care baby unit.

But while it was important to us to get the facts right, we were not a public information service.

We were a drama serial not a documentary, and having done our research and made sure we knew where we were coming from, we would then use the facts to mould our own stories. Tell them the way we wanted to.

And if, to suit one of our storylines, one of our characters didn't get the facts right, as happens so much in real life, that's the way we would play it.

Even though, on occasion, it didn't make us too popular with certain people.

One such case was when we had Eddie Yeats giving advice to Stan Ogden about social security payments – the wrong advice as it happened, to suit the storyline.

Next day we had the DSS on the phone to ask us to put it right at some stage.

They had been inundated with phone calls from folk wanting to know how they put in a claim based on what Eddie Yeats had told Stan, as they thought that they would qualify for the same benefits too.

When the DSS had tried to explain to the disillusioned callers that Eddie was wrong, they would have none of it. They were more ready to believe what Eddie had to say than the authorities.

We explained that the correct information would be forthcoming in the next episode, which made the DSS happier about the situation – but not the hundreds of people who thought they were in for a windfall at the taxpayers' expense!

And we were constantly having to remind folk that if the opinionated Percy Sugden, who had strong views on just about every subject under the sun, and particularly about 'authority' in whatever form it took, gave his forthright views about the local council, or said what he thought about the police force after his latest brush with the arm of the law, it was the opinion of Percy Sugden, one of our characters – not an official viewpoint being expressed by Granada Television!

Coronation Street was so convincing, our characters so true to life, that we would be constantly bombarded by organisations and special interest groups for publicity – anything, from a mention in a conversation, to displaying a poster or a collecting box in the Rovers or putting products on display behind the bar or in the corner shop, none of which could we do at that time.

There was one occasion however, when it was agreed that we could promote something that was deemed to be in the public interest.

The Royal Mint were introducing a new coin, and they felt the most effective way of familiarising the public with it was through *Coronation Street*.

If we could have two characters discussing the coin in the Rovers, it would be of tremendous help in letting our viewers, who numbered a fair section of the adult population, know exactly what it looked like. So that is what we did.

But as we recorded some three weeks ahead of transmission, we had to have the coin before it was generally released to the public.

And the Royal Mint went to extraordinary lengths to ensure security. They sent the coin up to Manchester from South Wales with a security guard. He was on set every minute the coin was out of his hands, and he never took his eyes off it. As soon as the scene had been shot, back he went to South Wales.

And the value of the coin that had been cloaked in such security at such considerable expense?

Twenty pence!

29

IT STARTED WITH A PARSNIP

THERE WAS MANY an occasion when the media helped to stoke this feeling among the public that our characters and their situations really existed.

They would regularly latch on to a storyline, or a character's behaviour or dilemma and run columns of advice to those concerned.

It may be advice on matters as diverse as finance, gardening, do-it-yourself, or on personal matters and relationships – some newspapers even brought their agony aunts into the front line.

Anything they could latch on to, they did.

And why not? It was the most popular show on television. The characters were like family to millions.

And we didn't object. It made their lives all that much more believable far beyond the television screen.

One of the comic stories we played that had a tremendous impact beyond the cobbles of *Coronation Street* was between Derek and Mavis, in which Mavis had read in a magazine that if you wanted to spice up your love life, parsnips was the answer.

So she started to feed them to Derek in various forms for practically every meal.

The papers took up the discussion as to the supposed effects of parsnips and other root vegetables on the human libido. And the price started to creep up and up. It was even reported regularly on radio. Eventually, the inevitable happened – there was a national shortage and the price rocketed as thousands of viewers followed Mavis's example.

I don't remember seeing any reports of a peak in the birth

rate some nine months later, but I do hope our viewers who were diligently following every step of the story had more success in achieving their aims than Mavis did!

One of the biggest impacts ever made by a storyline in *Coronation Street* was by the Ken/Deirdre/Mike triangle storyline, where Mike attempting to entice Deirdre away from Ken, had an affair with her and begged her to leave her husband for him. It turned into a dramatic will-she-or-won't-she scenario, with viewers pretty much divided over what they thought the outcome would and should be.

Even those who were not regular viewers of *Coronation Street* couldn't escape the national debate.

There was something in the national press every day. All manner of advice was given by a variety of experts through the columns of just about every newspaper in the land.

The church aired its views on the situation, as did psychiatrists, doctors and marriage guidance counsellors.

Bookies were revising odds on the outcome daily.

Computers were fed with the details of the affair in an attempt to try to determine the most likely outcome.

On the night the matter was resolved, one theatre was reported to have abandoned a performance as only one ticket had been sold, and a town council adjourned it's meeting until after eight o'clock, as a record number of viewers tuned in to see Deirdre decide to stay with Ken.

It was even flashed up on the scoreboard at Old Trafford at half time during the Manchester United v Arsenal match to a resounding cheer from over 50,000 fans!

I am often asked how well I knew the cast.

If they were referring to the actors, I knew them all. We worked together. Some we socialised with, some we didn't. With one or two, deep friendships developed. But I wouldn't say that I knew many of them really well.

But if they were referring to the characters they played in *Coronation Street*, I knew them better than I knew my own family.

I had to if I was to make them believable to close on 20 million viewers, because so many of them would share some characteristic or other with one of our stars on screen, or know someone who did.

If I went into a bar with my own sister, I would have to ask her what she wanted to drink. I would have no idea.

But if I went into a pub with Mike Baldwin. I would know he would have a large scotch. That's what he drank. Get that wrong and I would have half the television viewers in Britain on my neck!

Drink in the Rovers, by the way, was usually shandy, cola or apple juice. It had to be. You can imagine the state Mike Baldwin would have been in drinking large scotches if we had to do several takes of a bar scene or two!

The casting of the characters has always been extremely important in establishing and maintaining that unbridled belief that what was happening on screen was indeed an extension to the viewer's own life, their own world.

Any new character would be discussed at story conference in considerable depth between the writers and the production team, and, most importantly, the casting director.

As the discussions progressed, the casting director would get a feel for the emerging picture of the newcomer, and such was their knowledge of the business and the actors who worked within it, that before the discussions finished, they would probably have at least a couple of candidates in mind.

During the story conference, anyone round the table may come up with a suggestion, maybe an actor whose work they were familiar with, or someone they knew. All things were considered.

If a fairly clear picture emerged during the day, which more often than not it did, an availability check would be carried out by the casting director, so there was a good chance that by the end of the conference, everyone would know if a particular actor or actors were available for the episodes under discussion.

They would then be invited in for audition. If the auditions didn't work out as expected, it was back to the drawing board.

A lot of hard work went into the development of any new character before they ever hit our screens. The finished product was a result of the combined efforts of casting, writer, director, producer and of course what the actor themselves brought to the role.

It was a tried and trusted system, and in the majority of cases, gave us exactly what we were looking for.

The ongoing development of that character on screen was part of the magic, the chemistry created between actor, writer and director.

If they got it right, the character survived and flourished. If not, it was an early exit.

I've seen it from both sides – the character who was brought into the show with a long run in mind, only to be written out very quickly because it was obviously not working; and the character who was brought in for a couple of episodes and made such an impact that he or she was still there years later.

One such actor was Geoffrey Hughes, who came in initially for three episodes to play bin man Eddie Yeats and ended up staying with us for eight years!

He made such a tremendous impact and sparked so many stories through his inter-action with other Street regulars, in particular with Stan and Hilda Ogden, the character was pure gold.

Many of his exploits became television classics.

The introduction of the mural in the Ogdens' living room – her 'muriel', as Hilda called it – was a prime example.

That came about when Eddie was looking for accommodation, and in return for a room he offered to decorate Stan and Hilda's living room.

He bought the paper cheap from a fire salvage sale. But he didn't have enough to finish the job, and he couldn't get any more. So to cover the shortfall, he stuck a huge mural on one wall, convincing Hilda it was the latest fashion.

Within days of the episode hitting the screen, there was hardly a mural to be bought anywhere. They'd all been snapped up by eager viewers wanting to emulate Hilda's lakeland scene.

And her ducks in flight became legend.

Another classic comedy moment came when Eddie convinced Stan that a good way of cleaning his chimney was to tie a brick to the end of a length of clothes line and drop it down.

Only one chimney looked the same as any other to Stan in a row of terraced houses, and he dropped the brick down the wrong one – giving Elsie Tanner the fright of her life!

Then there was the time that Eddie convinced Annie Walker that he could get her a new personally monogrammed carpet for the Rovers hall, stairs and landing. He assured her that it would have her initials AW tastefully woven into it, which would without doubt establish her superior station in life.

Annie was delighted – until she next went to the cinema and found that Eddie had landed her with some off-cuts from the Astoria, Weatherfield!

The character of Eddie Yeats was a fine example of the influence of Bill Podmore, who worked on the show for over a decade as producer and executive producer and who brought his comedy background to the show in a big way.

Eddie Yeats was originally a bit of an unsavory character skulking on the edge of the law before becoming the loveable rogue who was to give us so many comedy stories during his long run with the show.

As Bill steered the programme more towards comedy, some of the most memorable double acts in its history began to flourish as a result of the developing storylines – Stan and Hilda, Rita and Mavis, Mavis and Derek, Bet and Alec, and so it went on.

Bill Podmore had joined Granada Television as a cameraman before becoming a director, working mainly on comedy. One of the shows he directed was *Nearest and Dearest* on which his friend John Stevenson was one of the writers, and it was to herald a partnership that was to bring so many memorable comedy moments to television.

Bill produced and directed John's *Last of the Baskets* and *How's Your Father*, and when he took over as producer of *Coronation Street* in 1976, he soon had John on the writing team.

It turned out to be a move that was to play a major part in bringing out new aspects of many of our characters as their comedy potential was explored to the full.

Bill was also responsible for bringing together the comedy talent of John and fellow *Coronation Street* writer Julian Roach when they wrote *Corrie* spin off *The Brothers McGregor* and also the highly-acclaimed *Brass,* set in a northern mill town and starring Timothy West, on which Bill was executive producer.

Bill Podmore was involved with *Coronation Street* as either producer or executive producer for some 12 years from 1976 until his retirement in 1988. He was proud of the fact that on many an occasion, due in no small part to his influence, *Corrie* was dubbed the best half hour of comedy on television.

That was not to mean that it was all comedy. It wasn't. There was a whole range of dramatic stories, the shooting of Ernie Bishop in a bungled wages raid on the warehouse being one. And for me, one of the most moving and memorable scenes was Hilda returning alone to her home to open the brown paper parcel containing Stan's possessions after he had passed away.

Bill passed away in 1994, having made one of the greatest contributions to entertainment during his years with ITV.

He is another man I have been privileged to have known and to have worked with, a man of great personality whose time with *Coronation Street* is remembered as one of the golden eras of the show.

30

FROM SCRIPT TO SCREEN

AFTER THE STORY conference, the writers went away to work on the episode they had been commissioned to write the week before, while the storyline writers got on with their task of making some order out of what had been discussed at conference.

And how long did we have to write an episode of *Coronation Street*?

Depending on where it came in the cycle, between 10 days and two weeks.

And how long did we need?

Every minute that we had.

And it was at this stage when those words that are etched in every writer's brain really came home to roost.

'No experience is ever wasted.'

Whether it be a situation, a chance meeting, an overheard conversation or even the characteristics of someone you knew well, it was all grist to the mill when it came to writing your script.

All this experience ensures that you base what you are writing on real people, real situations that your audience will believe in. You're job is to be original, not just to recycle what you have seen or read in the media.

There really are people out there whose total knowledge of a particular subject is based only on what they have seen in some television drama, heard on the radio or read in the press.

That is not to say there are not some excellent programmes being made and articles being written which greatly enhance people's knowledge and present an accurate picture. But it is someone else's picture – not a canvas that has been painted by you.

One aspect of my work that I really looked forward to was the technical run, the rehearsal on Wednesday afternoons on the week of recording where the actors went through the entire episode without scripts for the benefit of the director, his PA, producer, lighting, camera and sound crews, props, and the numerous other technical support staff without whom the programme would never have got off the ground.

The hard work of physically writing the script, the editing, the conversations with the director over what exactly I had in mind when I wrote certain words or scenes, were all over and done with. This was the moment of truth. The scenes, the speeches, every word that I had carefully crafted were about to come to life as the cast went through the episode for timing and other last minute notes. This was when the dream became reality. When the scenes that I had pictured in my imagination at the time I put the first words on the page would come alive.

In the days before the construction of the purpose-built Stage One, a self-contained *Coronation Street* studio complex with the major sets permanently erected, the tech run was acted out on a floor of the Granada office building.

Walls, doors and furniture were marked out on the floor with tape. This was because that with so many other programmes in production, the *Coronation Street* sets couldn't be erected in the studio until the night before the first recording day. So although the tech run served its purpose from a technical point of view, which of course was the whole point of the exercise, there wasn't the same magic about the scenes coming to life as there was when we were able to see them in the actual sets that would be seen on screen.

But Stage One changed all that and apart from the improved facilities, dressing rooms, privacy and relaxation areas for the cast and production staff, it provided a much more realistic view of how the show would eventually look.

I always used to attend the technical run when one of my episodes was in production mainly for a couple of reasons. Firstly, for the sheer joy of seeing my work leap off the page to become reality, and secondly, because I was on hand to answer any queries from the cast or director, and to clarify any points they may wish to raise.

I was also on hand to make any cuts should they be needed – or, heaven forbid, come up with something to fill the gaps left by an under run.

I used to pride myself that in the majority of cases, my scripts ran pretty well to time. I discovered fairly early in my career that an ITV half hour never was as long as a BBC half hour because of the need to accommodate the commercials.

If the episode came out anything round about a minute or so short, that would usually take care of itself by 'spreading' during the actual recording. Anything up to a couple of minutes over, could often be accommodated by tightening at the recording or editing stage.

But anything outside these fairly constrained parameters amounted to an over run or an under run which would need some sort of corrective action.

The truth would be revealed as the writers sat expectantly in the Rovers bar set after the tech run with the producer and the PA as she totted up the individual scene timings before announcing the good or bad news.

The over run was the easier to handle. Very rarely did a whole scene have to go. Usually a topping and tailing of the odd scene would do the trick. But an under run was a different proposition.

Do we extend an additional scene? Do we write a new one? Either way it meant a rapid decision so that the members of the cast involved could be told, while the writer feverishly took up his or her pen to go to work, sometimes with quite unforeseen consequences.

I remember an episode of mine that came out at some two and a half minutes under. I needed to come up with a way of filling the gap without losing the overall pace and rhythm of the main storylines. So I opted to write some additional words that would fairly comfortably extend a scene in the Rovers, in which other action was taking place, so there would be no loss of dramatic impetus.

I had noticed some time before as I drove to Granada studios a public house called the Ox Noble on Liverpool Road, and I had been intrigued enough by the name to do a bit of research into where it had come from. I discovered that it was in fact the name of a potato that had its origins in Lincolnshire in the mid-19th century, where it had been grown principally for animal feed.

So what was its connection with Manchester? One version of the story suggested that the potato had been introduced by the many men from that part of the country who had come to the area to work on the construction of the Liverpool-Manchester railway, which was opened in 1830, or in the construction of the Manchester Ship Canal some years later.

Another account indicated that it had been just one of a number of varieties brought into the city for sale in the market halls which at the time were situated on the other side of Liverpool Road to the public house.

Either way, it gave me the basis of a scene between Ken Barlow and a newly-arrived resident on the street, in which the stranger inquired about the origin of the name of our Rovers Return, which led into a discussion about unusual pub names in general. The Ox Noble was mentioned, and the newcomer wondered if Ken had any idea of the origin of that, with it being so unusual.

Of course, Ken, as now, did have something to say on the subject, as he does on the subject of most things of high importance, and with a couple of interjections from Betty, it made a nice little cameo to fill the gap. And that, I thought, was that.

But I reckoned without the intense interest in all things *Coronation Street* by our viewers.

The correspondence seemed to go on for weeks as viewers regaled us with tales not only of the origins of unusual pub names, the history of every variety of potato under the sun but also memories of long departed forebears who had worked on the Liverpool-Manchester railway, the Manchester Ship Canal or the markets in Liverpool Road.

At the end of it all, Ken Barlow wasn't the only expert!

31

WHEN THE BEST LAID PLANS . . .

My approach to writing the characters was simple. I would look at every situation through their eyes, from their point of view, and write every word of dialogue accordingly.

To help me to do this when I first started, I had a set of cast photographs, and I would have in front of me pictures of whoever was in the scene I was currently writing.

After a while, I didn't need this because I knew the characters as well as my own family. I only had to type a name on a page, and just about every aspect of that character loomed large in my mind.

And it was always important to remember that television is a visual medium. It is not just talking heads. An expression, a glance could be worth a dozen words.

And frequently, a reaction shot could be just as effective, even more so, than the camera being on the person delivering the speech.

Harry Kershaw always used to reckon that in a good *Coronation Street* script, you should be able to cover the names above the dialogue and know who the lines were meant for.

I have often been asked the difference between the roles of the producer and the director.

Broadly speaking, the producer is responsible for controlling everything that goes on behind the cameras – the writers, the casting, the day to day running of the show. While the director's job is to bring the printed word from the page into dramatic life on the screen by directing the cast, the cameras, the sound, the lighting at his disposal to bring about the most effective result.

So when the producer had read your script, talked through any preliminary edits he or she may want doing, it was passed through to the director, with the other episodes that were being recorded in the same week.

When your script had passed into the director's hands and preparation started in earnest, there would inevitably be more fine tuning as attitudes and moods of the characters became more rounded.

Everything was moulded, polished and prepared for the week of recording, so that nothing was left to chance.

Of course, there were times when things didn't go according to plan, but these were usually taken in the stride of the very professional production crew, without whom the show would never have happened and for whom I always had the highest regard.

I have played golf with many of them over many years , and surprisingly when you get to know them away from the pressures of studio life, some of them are almost human!

For the most part, many minor setbacks and glitches didn't come to the notice of the writer, but there were times when an actor fell ill, or had a personal emergency to deal with, and some last minute adjustments to the script were needed.

And if the emergency happened during the actual week of recording, you were well and truly in the front line.

The most testing time for me started with a phone call one Sunday evening. I was in the car on the M6 as Avril and I were returning from a weekend in Stratford-upon-Avon.

It was the producer, who wanted to know where I was. When I told him, he told me not to worry, but to ring him when I got home.

Now when the producer of *Coronation Street* rings you

on your car phone at half past seven on Sunday evening and asks how long it will be before you get home, believe me, you worry.

When I got in I rang him. He told me that one of our actors had been taken into hospital and there was no way he was going to take any part in that week's recording.

Now if luck had been on my side, it would have been someone who had two lines in the café or corner shop, or a brief exchange in the Rovers.

No chance. It was an actor who was central to the main story, and he was involved in almost half the scenes being recorded that week – and for which filming started first thing the following morning.

So what did we do?

I contacted Paul Abbot, the other writer whose scripts were in studio that week, and we discussed possible storyline ideas to fill the gap, We eventually came up with one that involved three additional members of the cast who had been written out that week, meaning that they were available if needed. I then phoned the producer back, ran through the new story thread, which he was happy with, and told him which characters we wanted in the morning. Our priority at that time was to write the film scenes which were being recorded the following day.

He rang the three actors we needed and told them to turn up on the film location the following morning, while Paul and I got to work.

I was up until three o'clock in the morning. I've no idea how long it took Paul, – but we had our new film scenes on set by half past seven, recording got underway and the remainder of the re-written scenes duly arrived in time for them to be learned by the actors, blocked by the director and to take their place in the rest of the week's production schedule.

And I would guarantee that if it hadn't been for the fact that the actor's illness and 'Crisis for Corrie' had been extensively reported in the National press. when the shows were transmitted not one viewer would have been able to tell where we had to do the running repairs.

It was a remarkable example of how the writers, cast, director and production team had such an understanding of how each other worked that we were able to come together under such circumstances and produce such a polished, finished product.

32

MISTAKES? WHAT MISTAKES?

CONTINUITY IS ALWAYS something that has to be carefully watched to make sure that there are no unscheduled dramatic changes between one scene and another, whether it be wardrobe, props or some other aspect of studio dressing.

The studio interiors and the exterior scenes were rarely filmed in sequence. Quite often an exterior may be filmed on the Sunday or Monday, while the interior scenes to be screened before it and after it would not be shot until the following Thursday or Friday, so there were many chances for a slip to be made.

The classic, of course, was to ensure that if it had been raining outside when the exterior was filmed, when a character went indoors, they looked as if they had actually been in the rain and were not just returning from a Caribbean holiday, even if the two scenes were recorded days apart.

Incidentally if you've ever wondered how we managed to get rain on demand – yes, even in Manchester we needed some assistance on occasion – the answer was simple. We called in the help of the fire brigade!

We had to be careful that our characters were wearing the same clothes and looked the same when they walked out of one scene and into another, though they may be shot three or four days apart. And we had to ensure that props were the same and all placed in the same position as when we had last seen them.

And if we did make the odd mistake, we could be just as inventive in coming up with an explanation as our eagle-eyed viewers could be in spotting it.

On one occasion, Jim Macdonald brought in two mugs of coffee, and put one down for himself and one for Liz.

When we came back to the scene after the advertising break, which hadn't been shot in sequence for technical reasons, the mugs had been switched round.

It was spotted of course by one of our viewers, who was delighted to think she had caught us out.

But we explained that Jim took sugar and Liz didn't, and he had put the mugs down the wrong way round. As soon as he had tasted his drink (during the advertising break) he realised his mistake and swopped them over!

Wardrobe is a big responsibility in any drama production, particularly, of course, those set in a different period. *Coronation Street* was no exception. It didn't matter whether the actor or actress favoured a particular way of dressing. What mattered to the show was that the character was dressed realistically for the part they were playing.

In fact, wardrobe is so important to some actors that they don't feel properly in character until they have some particular article of clothing, or personal prop. It may have been Albert Tatlock's threadbare suit, Percy Sugden's cap, Deirdre's spectacles, Hilda's pinny – something that had become a trade mark of that particular person in the show.

Some of the characters wouldn't even go on set unless they had a favourite article of clothing or prop.

Every major character had at least three sets of clothes – working, casual and Sunday best. And if you wonder where we managed to find such a range of clothing that looked so authentic for every principal member of the cast, quite often wardrobe needed to look no further than the nearest charity shop.

I am often asked what role the floor manager has in a television production. Is he or she responsible for sweeping up afterwards? Do they have to make sure the studio floor is litter-free?

Not quite. The floor manager in any television production is the vital link between the director, who is in the control room with his team seeing everything on a number of television screens, and the cast on the studio floor.

The floor manager has to make sure that everything is as it should be for recording – and above all, he has to be the soul of discretion.

When, after the third take of a particular scene, the exasperated director screams down to his floor manager 'Tell that mindless idiot that if he doesn't get it right this time I'll have him strung up by his b***s' the floor manager will convey the message to the studio floor by saying 'Sorry, chaps. We'll have to go again. Technical problem upstairs.'

As the actors got older, so their limitations became more pronounced. It was a problem we always knew we would come up against eventually. Many members of the cast were approaching or already past normal retirement age when they first came into the show.

So we wrote their parts bearing this in mind.

When they found it more difficult to remember long speeches, we didn't write them any more. We kept their words and their appearances down to a minimum. And because we knew them so well, were familiar with every little nuance of their character which we had built up and nurtured over the years, we were able to do it without ever diminishing the strength of the character. Or, most important, the dignity of the actor.

With some actors, what was seen on screen wasn't the whole story.

There was a time when we cast an aging music hall star in a role. The man in question seemed just right for it. He got through the audition without a problem, but when we got down to the serious business of his actually playing the part for which he had been cast, we discovered that he had a fairly serious failing – he had great difficulty remembering his lines. So we ended up shooting most of his scenes with his words written on cards held up in his eye line, out of shot of the cameras!

It was never intended that it would be a long-runner in story terms. Needless to say, the part we had written for him became even more short-lived.

With the sheer number of words in a drama serial, not everyone could learn and remember lines at the same rate as others.

Many have little ways of their own to assist them to get their speeches right, but whatever way they choose, they do usually get there in the end.

There are occasions though, when an emergency arises and we have to resort to ingenuity.

On one occasion a short substitute scene had to be written just before recording was due to take place.

The characters involved had a quick sight of the new scene, but a couple of them needed the extra reassurance of some form of prompt.

The scene was in the Rovers bar, so a couple of the actors had written cue lines on beer mats on top of the bar.

At one point, a flustered Percy Sugden entered in some state of agitation, delivered a speech and went out again as quickly as he had come in.

Unfortunately, he did so with a flourish of his unzipped anorak – and cleared all the beer mats off the bar top.

On that occasion, we were all very relieved that the show was recorded and not going out live!

Initially, the exterior was a set in the studio. This was eventually replaced by a purpose-built outside lot on Grape

Street next to the Granada Television centre, but for various technical reasons, smaller than actual size.

This was for the most part of no significance, unless we had to use a large vehicle, such as a motor coach or a fire engine, which could stretch practically the length of the street. You could almost get on a bus at the back outside the Rovers and get off again at the front outside the corner shop without the bus actually moving!

This outside lot was closed to the public, and the only way to get to walk the cobbles of the most famous Street in the world at that time was to make an appointment for someone connected with the show to take you round.

This was something I did on many occasions.

My party piece was to tell the visitors which character lived in which house, which seemed to go down well as we meandered our way along the cobbles.

Until the day I was asked to take some visitors from New Zealand round the set.

I did my preamble, unlocked the gates and let them take in the reality of physically being on the set of their favourite television show, a moment that they had travelled from the other side of the world to savour., They spent some time taking photographs of each other before we started our leisurely stroll from the Rovers Return to the Corner Shop. My big moment had arrived as we drew level with each house. Number one, Albert, Ken and Deirdre; number three Emily; number five Bert and Ivy Tilsley...

By the time I got to the end, I was greeted by a sea of puzzled faces.

They were watching *Coronation Street* in New Zealand five years behind us. They hadn't heard of nearly half the cast!

At the beginning of the 1980s, the site was wanted for development by Granada Studios Tour, and a new *Coronation*

Street exterior, now much nearer full size, was built just a few yards away.

The new set was officially opened in May 1982 by Her Majesty the Queen and the Duke of Edinburgh, who were among the first people to walk along the famous cobbles that were to grace our television screens for many years to come.

And the newly-built set must have been a great relief to Albert Tatlock,

Albert lived at No 1, next door to the Rovers. On the new set, there was an alleyway between the Rovers and No 1.

But on the original set, there wasn't.

And as was pointed out to us on many occasions, the door to the toilets in the Rovers was on the wall adjoining No 1.

So every time anyone went through that door, the only place they could have ended up was in Albert Tatlock's kitchen, and as more than one viewer observed it did make you wonder what they were doing in Albert's sink.

Whatever it was, it could have been the reason for his trademark downcast expression!

This new exterior set, as well as being used for location work, went on to form an integral part of the Granada Studios Tour for many years, and visitors from all over the world were able to walk up and down it, taking each other's photographs leaving or entering one of the most famous pubs in television history.

When the show was 40 years old, I actually produced a souvenir edition of the *Weatherfield Recorder*.

It was a dream for me – four pages of stories about our characters, their lives and local issues, something I had done for real many years before when I was working in local weekly newspapers.

Only on this occasion I could make it all up without any fear of comeback from my readers!

For weeks after its publication, I used to see visitors to the Tours outside the Kabin, waiting for it to open so they could buy a paper.

It was one more example of the inter-action and close blurring of the lines between the fictitious world of *Coronation Street* and its inhabitants and the reality accepted by the viewers the show served so faithfully.

Writing for *Coronation Street* was an experience that I was fortunate enough to enjoy for almost 30 years.

I worked with some of the most talented people in the entertainment business, both on screen and behind the scenes, many of whom became close personal friends and whose company I still enjoy to this day.

It has been a great privilege and, for me, totally unforgettable.

33

OCCASIONALLY, I HAD A PROPER JOB!

ALTHOUGH I WAS a member of the *Coronation Street* script-writing team, from time to time I did have a proper job, much to the relief of my mother, God bless her, who used to regularly ask if I was at home, or if I was working. There was no way she could have possibly envisaged that the two situations could be one and the same.

And the 'proper job' meant arriving at the television studios at nine thirty in the morning and working office hours until about six o'clock, five days a week. It happened when I was called in to stand in for one of the regular storyline writers, who week in, week out constructed the *Corrie* storylines around which the scripts were built. I would usually be working with Tom Elliott or Diane Culverhouse, both very experienced writers and not only in television. Tom was an award-winning writer for the theatre, while Diane had joined the team with a distinguished career in radio to her credit.

The storyline writers' contribution to the nuts and bolts of the show was tremendous. They picked up the story points that had been thrown onto the table at story conferences and put them into a more detailed form broken down scene by scene that would provide a pretty firm outline for the next episodes to be commissioned. They also fed in their additional touches where there was a need to maintain the balance between drama and humour, comedy and pathos.

Story conference, held every three weeks usually on a Monday, was attended by all the writers, the producer, their secretary, archivist and casting director, as well as the storyline writers. When the storyline writers got to the office on the Tuesday morning following story conference, the first thing we did was to summarise the story points, allocating them through the number of episodes we were working on, and firming up the key scenes that took us into the advertising breaks and ends of episodes.

Then we had the task of finalising the cast list. Everyone at the story conference had been made aware of those cast members who were available and those who were not. But we still had to decide who, as well as the principal characters, we would need to play the stories. Who did we have to use because they were behind with the number of episodes they had been guaranteed? And which of the other available members of the cast could we get best value out of for peripheral stories?

Then we would discuss the availability of film, how we could best use it, and the interior sets we would need to best tell the stories, as for many years we were restricted on the number of interior sets we could get into the studio.

Would we get better value out of the corner shop or the garage? The newsagent's or the betting shop? The hairdresser's or the cafe? As I have previously mentioned, with the eventual building of Stage One, the dedicated *Coronation Street* studio complex, the set restrictions were eased considerably as we had many more sets permanently erected.

So having established the required sets, allocated use of film and assigned the story threads to each episode that we were working on, we could start writing: Scene One. Int. Rovers Living Room, 0900.

At this point, with the basic blueprint provided by the story conference in front of us, we would quickly blend into the world of our characters as we started the job of constructing each episode in more detail, scene by scene.

The days didn't go without interruptions, which were usually always welcome. They provided moments of light relief. Our cast members and the other entertainers who were around the studios at that time appearing in a variety of other star-studded award-winning shows from *Stars in Their Eyes* to *Sherlock Holmes*, local news programmes to *The Comedians*, were affable folk and with very few exceptions, good company.

Sue Nicholls may pop in to show us some creation she had bought at lunchtime, Liz Dawn would stick her head round the door to let us know that toilet rolls were on offer at Tesco. Thelma Barlow would discuss the book that she had just collected on her lunchtime shopping trip. Peter Baldwin would update us on the latest acquisitions for his toy emporium in Covent Garden. Or they may just drop in hoping for a quick clandestine glance at our chart indicating when we would be using them in future episodes.

Colin Crompton, Ken Goodwin, Duggie Brown – brother of Lynn Perrie, our Ivy – or one of the other comedians would come to regale us with their latest gags during a break from rehearsals for their show. Or dear Leslie Crowther, who was presenting *Stars in Their Eyes* at the time, would just wander in for a cup of tea, the conversation almost inevitably turning before long to the subject of his beloved cricket.

It was a strange world, but totally enjoyable to see behind the facade of so many well-known faces, to spend precious moments with them as just ordinary folk relaxing and enjoying the times when they could put their public persona to one side and just be themselves.

And the public persona was generally dropped completely in the Festival Café, where we would find ourselves sharing a table with local programmes presenters, continuity announcers, members of our cast or an actor or two who happened to be recording at GTV at the time.

While we were having lunch in either the café or the Stables across the road from the studio, we were just work colleagues chatting about all manner of subjects from our families to where you could buy the cheapest petrol, what was on television the night before, or the latest efforts to give up smoking.

For some actors this wasn't the case, particularly if they were working on a major production. From the moment they entered the building, they would assume the character of whoever they were there to play at the time, and it seemed to stay with them until they left. I suspect in some of the more extreme cases, it continued far beyond the studios of Granada Television.

Fridays were different. Recording was taking place. Our cast were all made up and in costume at lunchtime, and Granada laid on a lavish buffet for them in one of the committee rooms, where we would join them. It was always time well spent for me, because it provided time to not only talk about the show but to get to know them more informally. This helped to see them in a different light and could often bring a new dimension to their character, which could be used when writing for them.

These informal meetings were particularly useful when we were meeting a new member of the cast for the first time, whether they were in the show for the long haul or just a few episodes.

The characters in *Coronation Street* were moulded by not only what the actor brought to the role, but the input, too, of the writer, director and producer; and the better I came to know the actor, the more facets I was able to bring to the character, subtle as they may be, one more step in making them totally believable for our viewers.

I used to find storyline writing for *Coronation Street* invaluable, not only in giving me a deeper understanding and insight into how the show was run, but in understanding the problems of other people on the show, whether they be producer, cast member, director, PA. stage manager, wardrobe or any other member of our company. And I think it made me a more understanding and sympathetic writer as a result.

We had to be true to our characters, see each situation from their point of view and believe in them implicitly. Because if we didn't, what chance was there of convincing the viewer?

Whether I was writing script or storyline, the characters were truly as real to me as close relatives. They may have been fictitious but they were as much a part of my life as they were of the lives of our viewers.

And there was the great advantage that when I had had enough of them, I could end the scene and move into someone else's world.

It was a wonderful, magical kingdom of make believe, but at the same time a carefully crafted piece of contemporary drama, with characters that viewers could not only believe in but have feelings for.

And that always has been and always will be what *Coronation Street* is all about.

34

FROM BASIL BRUSH TO BOOGIE WOOGIE

A CONSTANT SOURCE of great delight to me, working for *Coronation Street*, was the number of great friends I made at Granada TV in other areas of the business, and the opportunities that came my way to work with such a diverse range of producers, directors, actors and entertainers.

As a result, I was to write a variety of other shows, many of them for school and pre-school audiences, together with numerous reading books to go with them.

And to meet two producers who were to become firm and close friends for many years. They were John Coop and Pat Baker. Both were charming, gentle people from totally different backgrounds, sadly, both no longer with us.

John had been in primary school education and had moved into television from the headmastership of a village school in Cheshire.

Pat, with her husband Barry, had been one of the pioneers of ITV and was steeped in the television business. Pat and John were two of the most warm and totally genuine people I have ever met, and it has been one of the great pleasures of my life to have known and worked with them.

I first met John through Harry Kershaw, who told me that a producer in the education department was looking for a writer to work with him on a series he was making with Terry Hall and featuring Lenny the Lion. I joined John's little team and I have lost count of the number of series featuring a variety of entertainers and presenters we eventually did make, but they amounted to well in excess of 100 programmes.

And I first met Pat through John – who told me that there was a lady producer who was looking for a writer to work with on a new series! That led to me writing well over 100 shows for pre-school audiences, as well as *Dance Crazy* for tea-time audiences.

Another person I met at that time, who was also to become a good friend, was someone I admired for his talent as much as anyone I ever met during my years in the entertainment business.

He was Derek Hilton, Granada's musical director, whose role with the company was so wide-ranging and diverse, from writing music, providing backing tracks, playing piano accompaniment for a range of international stars to directing a full orchestra. I worked with Derek on many shows, and his skills never ceased to amaze me.

We co-wrote a number of signature tunes together. We would meet up in the sound studio, Derek at the piano, me with the words I wanted to put music too. He would glance through the words I presented him with, would invariably pick up the mood immediately and trot something out on his piano that more often than not was exactly what we were looking for. A couple of minor adjustments to the words by me to make them scan with the music, and we had it.

He could turn his hand and brilliant brain to anything musical. I got first hand experience of his versatility when he wrote and produced the title music for *Dance Crazy*, the musical series we produced which traced the history of dance crazes through the 20th century.

He brought a girl vocalist and three musicians into the studio, and aided and abetted by the wizardry of the sound engineer, created a superb 12 track recording, starting with his piano, and ending with the girl harmonising with her own voice. The perfect opening and closing music for *Dance Crazy* featured not only the instruments and vocals, but all manner of special effects to enhance the experience, from seagull calls to hand claps.

This was before the days of computers and multi-instrument keyboards. All the sounds had to be produced by the individual instruments. And it was just another day at the office for Derek, one of the truly great talents of the music scene. Sadly, he passed on some years ago. He is sadly missed.

It was while working on *Dance Crazy* that the skills and invaluable contribution of the musical director were again brought home to me. When our MD for the show – not Derek this time – wasn't working with us, he was working in pantomime at Bradford. He would come over to rehearsals, run through the numbers on the piano with principals Billy Boyle and Lesley Judd, go back home to Yorkshire and by the beginning of the following week, be back with a dozen band parts that he had hand written over the weekend! What a talent.

And it was while I was working on *Dance Crazy* that it was brought home to me just how competitive this business is, and to what lengths performers will go in their quest for work.

We were looking to take on six dancers for the show, the auditions being held in a room over a public house in Chiswick. Due to a mix-up on the tube – my mistake, not theirs – I arrived later than planned, to find the line of hopefuls stretching down the stairs, out of the door, along the street and around the corner. One girl had come from Newcastle on the coach, another from the Wirral. One of the boys was from Preston, another from Torquay. Were they fazed by all the competition? Not a bit of it. It was all part and parcel of chasing their dream. Auditions over, they would head back to

Victoria bus station for the long journey home to wait for the next glimmer of hope.

If there was anyone who deserved to succeed in the business, it was the boys and girls I met that day. They may have had their sights set on the stars, but what really mattered to them was to dance whenever and wherever the opportunity arose.

At one point, I was working on three shows for Granada at the same time, featuring Billy Boyle, Basil Brush and singer Mark Wynter. I first met them all in Plymouth, where, as it happened, they were all appearing together in pantomime. Billy was Basil's 'straight' man at that time.

I was writing *Dance Crazy* for Pat Baker, in which Billy was one of the stars; writing *Sounds Like a Story*, a pre-school series also for Pat, which was to be presented by Mark Wynter; and I was about to start work with John Coop on a series featuring Basil Brush.

Talk about variety being the spice of life. With *Coronation Street* also on the boil, it certainly was for me at that point in my career!

Mark had achieved fame many years before as a pop singer, his big hit being *Venus in Blue Jeans.* He is remarkable. To my knowledge, he has never been seriously out of work since his days of pop stardom, being in constant demand for just about every West End musical that has ever been staged.

I was to write many shows for Basil. Ivan Owen, his operator when I was writing for him, is sadly no longer with us, though Basil, of course, continues to be as popular as ever wherever he appears.

It was Ivan at that time who gave Basil his unmistakeable voice and laugh. The first time we met was in the theatre bar in Plymouth after a matinee performance. While everyone knew Mark Wynter and Billy Boyle from the pantomime, they didn't know Ivan without Basil – but they recognised the voice, and it was comical to see them looking all over the room for the unseen mischievous fox.

This was to become a regular occurrence over the next few months in restaurants and hotels up and down the country. When we were together, we never really stopped working, coming up with gags for Basil at every opportunity. We needed to. He got through them at an amazing rate on screen.

Whenever Ivan laughed, complete silence descended on the restaurant, or the bar or hotel lounge where we happened to be as the other customers tried to put a face to the well-known voice, then when recognition dawned, looked around to see where the little rascal was hiding.

Rehearsals for his shows could be quite riotous affairs, too, as we talked through scripts and ideas, and Ivan, full of enthusiasm came roaring in with some comment or other that was typical Basil.

On one occasion, we were working at the Granada TV offices in Golden Square in London when we stopped an important meeting which was being held in the room next door.

A tentative face appeared round the door and asked what time we would be breaking for lunch as they couldn't concentrate for listening to what we were up to!

Basil's character was infectious. When he wasn't performing he was always with us in spirit. He took over our lives.

John and I used to commute to London for rehearsals, and from the moment we met up in the train at Wilmslow station, we talked about nothing but ideas for the Basil shows. And it was the same on the return journey, which nearly got us, or more precisely me, into big trouble on one occasion.

On our way home from rehearsing with Ivan and Howard Williams, his co-presenter for the series, our heads were still in a spin and our imaginations were running riot as we boarded the Manchester Pullman.

John and I were still on a high as we finished dinner, when John came up with the thought of doing a sequence featuring space travel. At which point, my mind clicked into manic overdrive. It had been a long day.

'Asteroids.'

'Asteroids? What about them?'

'My Uncle Willie was a martyr to them. He had to go to the doctor, you know.'

'And what did the doctor do?'

'He gave him a suppository.'

I am sure that by now you can see where this is going.

I got to the punchline just as the steward was asking John if he had enjoyed his meal.

Bang on cue, I came out with 'For all the good it did him. He might as well have shoved it up his a**se'.

We continued the rest of the journey home in complete silence – and we never did make a programme about space travel!

35

HOW NICE – A PLAY FOR MUMMY

In earlier chapters I have given many examples of how television viewers confuse fiction with reality – and it isn't just television viewers.

I came across a perfect example shortly after we had made *Dance Crazy* with Billy Boyle and Lesley Judd.

Billy was appearing in London in a production of *The Rivals*, a restoration comedy by Richard Brinsley Sheridan. Avril and I went down to see the show.

The star was Patricia Routledge, the never-to-be forgotten Hyacinth Bucket in *Keeping Up Appearances*, who was playing Mrs Malaprop.

In *Keeping Up Appearances*, Hyacinth had an unseen son called Sheridan.

During the interval, we overheard two elderly ladies in front of us discussing the play in general and Patricia Routledge in particular.

Looking at the name on the front of the programme, one lady said to the other: 'Isn't it good of her son Sheridan to write this play for her.'

And her companion agreed!

Talking of Mrs Malaprop, our own Hilda Ogden was known to throw in the odd malapropism.

'I can say this without fear of contraception' was just one example that within weeks of it being broadcast had more less become established in everyday conversation, as did many other comments of hers. When Stan lost his job at the Rovers, she told everyone he'd been 'made repugnant', and perhaps one of her most quoted of all 'the world's your lobster'.

Hylda Baker, the comedy actress, was also known for it in her many comedy roles.

One day, she was in Granada studios in Manchester and had been watching the monitor screens, which were showing the studio recording of *Coronation Street,* when she heard Hilda Ogden come out with one of her malapropisms.

I was in producer Bill Podmore's office at the time. Within minutes, Hylda Baker came steaming in, demanding to know the name of that woman who was doing her 'mixed up words.'

Bill told her it was Hilda Ogden.

'I'll sue her,' raged the incensed Miss Baker.

'She's not the first one' Bill explained.

'It all started with Mrs Malaprop.'

'I'll sue her' said Hylda.

Bill tried to enlighten her further.

'Mrs Malaprop was a character in a play by Sheridan,' he said.

Not to be put off, the irate Hylda stormed:

'I'll sue him, an all!'

Our pre-school programmes were aimed at the under 5s. We took educational advice on the content and carefully prepared the programmes with the young audience in mind.

Even though I had written some 200 television shows for pre-school and schools audiences, and some 50 books to accompany them, an incident happened in Liverpool one Christmas that made me aware that, even with my experience, I could never be one hundred per cent sure who our audience were.

I had been working on *Hickory House*, the pre-school series featuring animated mophead Dusty and stuffed cushion,

Humphrey. The live presenters were Alan Rothwell and at that time, Louise Hall Taylor.

Alan was appearing in the Christmas show at Liverpool Playhouse and we had taken our families over to see the matinee.

Before we went to the theatre, we were walking past the Cavern Club, when two punks appeared in front of us walking in our direction. They would probably be in their late teens. Their hair was superglued on top of their heads like a couple of cock combs and they sported an assortment of pins, studs and chains through so many parts of their bodies that I was convinced that every time they had a drink, they would have leaked like a pair of colanders.

They would have been worth a fortune in a scrap yard. And to say they looked menacing was an understatement.

As they continued walking purposefully towards us, it became increasingly apparent that it was one of those occasions when discretion was definitely the better part of valour. We moved our families to the other side of the road as the gap between us and the punks narrowed.

They crossed over too, and continued to walk straight towards us. Eventually we were unable to avoid coming face to face with them as they blocked our path.

One of them looked pointedly at Alan, and said 'We know you.'

Alan assured them that they didn't.

But the lad persisted, breaking into a delighted smile.

'Yes we do. You're Humphrey Cushion's dad.'

It turned out that these two were among our most fervent fans!

When Alan told them that I was the writer of the show, it made their day. They stayed with us all the way to the theatre.

Humphrey Cushion and Dusty Mop were very popular

with the young children, and during a break in the TV series when I took a four-week sabbatical from the Daily Mirror, Alan and I with puppet master Barry Smith decided to take a live show based on the characters into the theatre.

And it was while we were doing that show that it was brought home to me that no matter how much planning you put into a project, you will always come up against the unexpected.

I had written and was co-producing and directing the show with Alan, who was the main attraction through his television appearances. Co-starring were Barry's Dusty Mop and Humphrey Cushion, and we were joined for the live performances by Jenny Burke, Louise being unavailable.

After two weeks rehearsal, we opened the tour at the Ashcroft Theatre in Croydon, and the second week was to be at the Forum Theatre in Manchester.

The show was well received at the Ashcroft. We were putting on two performances a day at eleven in the morning and three in the afternoon. Any minor niggles with sound and lighting were quickly ironed out, we had good notices from the press, good houses and we were all looking forward to the Forum, which is a much smaller, more intimate theatre.

But when we got there, sales of tickets for the first three days were to say the least disappointing.

We couldn't work it out. The show was a TV spin off, we had had good pre-publicity and the opening show again received good notices. Yet we had to cancel one of the shows on the Wednesday through lack of support.

We couldn't explain it. The theatre management couldn't explain it – but the tea lady could.

It was nothing to do with the show. There had been a funfair at the park over the weekend, and she told us that folk would have taken their children there. They were spent up.

'Just wait till Thursday, when they get paid,' she told us.

And she was right. Friday and Saturday we had to put on two additional shows to meet the demand.

So if you've any major decisions to make, whatever business you're in, you could do worse than ask the opinion of the tea lady!

36

AND FOLK COULD BE SO HELPFUL

CENTRAL TO THE *Humphrey Cushion Birthday Show* was a birthday party. For the birthday party we needed a birthday cake with candles. And we needed it to be fireproof.

It was at this point that I found it quite amazing how some folk just take anything in their stride.

I came up with the idea of covering a round biscuit tin with a well-known brand of filler coloured with cochineal, so I went to the local do-it-yourself shop to buy some.

When I found the right section, it soon became apparent that there wasn't just one type of filler, there were many different types for a variety of different household uses – interior and exterior, filler for walls, ceilings, drainpipes, gutters, wood, plastic, metal, and this shop stocked the lot.

While I was looking at the array of packets and containers in front of me contemplating my choice, a young lady came up to me and asked if she could help.

I told her that I was looking for some filler. She asked what it was for. Without thinking, I told her it was to ice a birthday cake.

As soon as I said it, I realised what a deranged fool she must be taking me for. But before I could apologise and explain the situation, she was one step ahead.

Without a moment's hesitation, she took down a brightly coloured packet, handed it to me and said:

'I think this is what you're looking for'!

I was working on a *Saturday Night Theatre* play for radio that had a plot centred on the smuggling of precious stones into the UK from Amsterdam via Hamburg.

I needed to know if there was anywhere in England that it would be possible, no matter how unlikely, to land a light aircraft without it attracting too much attention from the authorities. If there was a one per cent chance, that was good enough for me to justify my plotline.

So who better to ring than the Civil Aviation Authority.

At first they were understandably very wary. They wanted to know who was calling and why I was asking the question. There followed a couple more questions, which I was convinced were delaying tactics on their part while they traced the call, but when I explained that I was a writer working on a radio play for *Saturday Night Theatre* and gave a rough outline of the plot, the attitude changed completely.

I was put through to someone who I was assured had the knowledge and authority to answer my question, which he did. He didn't actually give me a list of airfields, or even one, but he did respond to my suggestions, in the negative for the most part. Eventually I got the information I was looking for. Mission accomplished.

Wishing me good luck with the play, he did ask one thing in return – could I make sure to let him know the date of transmission, when I knew it.

Which I was more than happy to do. And I was delighted to have a letter forwarded to me after the broadcast telling me how authentic he had found it. I was of course delighted to hear it.

When you become a professional writer, you look at life in a different way. And you have to believe implicitly in every character you write. Because if you don't there is no way you are going to make them believable to your audience.

I wrote a six-part radio series, *The Innovators,* for Piccadilly Radio in Manchester which, through a mixture of narration and dramatised documentary, told the story of a number of famous men and women for whom the North West had played a significant part in the development of their business or their careers.

One of the programmes dealt with the beginnings of the Marks and Spencer empire, starting with the young Michael Marks arriving in England from Russia.

He made his way to Leeds, where he knew there were people who would help him to find his feet. There he met the owner of a warehouse, Isaac Dewhurst, who helped the young Michael set himself up selling wares from a tray on street corners.

In 1894, after Michael became friendly with accountant Tom Spencer, the pair opened a market stall in Leeds market. The rest, as they say, is history. The north west connection was that the pair opened their first shop in Cheetham Hill, Manchester.

When recording was completed, the radio station sent a copy of the tape to Michael Marks' granddaughter.

I was delighted to have a letter from her passed on to me by the radio station in which she praised the authenticity of the play, saying that was exactly how it had happened.

I had based it on fact, of course, but I had invented about 75 per cent of it in order to create the mood and atmosphere of the time.

By the time I finished writing it, I was almost convinced myself that I had been with them every step of the way.

The reason for this was because I had thoroughly researched my characters, as I did with all my work, and came to know them almost as well as I knew members of my own family. Most importantly, I believed in them one hundred per cent. If I hadn't done that, I could never have written them so convincingly.

Working on the children's television shows was a much smaller scale operation than *Coronation Street*.

There were hardly any changes to the scripts when we got into studio. It wasn't mainly spoken dialogue, as it was with *Corrie*. There was a lot more business in the children's programmes. But timing was still of paramount importance.

During rehearsals, we timed and re-timed every show as accurately as we were able, so by the time we got round to recording, the production team and presenters could just get on with it without having to worry too much about how long they were taking. And it was amazing how often the programme came out within seconds of the time we were aiming for.

But sometimes the written words on the page could be taken <u>too </u>literally.

We were working on a series called *Once Upon a Time*. This was aimed at pre-school children – I emphasise 'aimed at' bearing in mind my previous encounter with the Liverpool lads who were among Humphrey Cushion's biggest fans – and featured a classic story around which was woven a bit of business, both educational and entertaining to the youngsters.

Our presenter had been seated on a log, from where he had told a story featuring a white rabbit. Towards the end of the show, he 'discovered' a white rabbit, that had supposedly escaped from its hutch. To close the show, he picked up the rabbit and made his exit as he took it back to its home.

Some programmes later, we had another story featuring a rabbit, and we again wanted to feature a live animal on the show. It was popular with the young viewers.

So this time, by way of a change and for no other reason, I specified a brown rabbit. The colour really was immaterial.

We contacted the man who supplied the animals to our shows, and he duly turned up with a box.

Just before recording, I went to look for him to tell him the rabbit would be needed in about ten minutes, and he opened the box to reveal the white rabbit. I pointed out that this time we had specified a brown rabbit. He said he didn't have a brown rabbit, but not to worry. Give him a few minutes and we wouldn't know the difference. And he brought out a tin of cocoa and prepared to sprinkle it all over the hapless bunny.

I quickly stopped him, and told him it didn't matter what colour the rabbit was – but we certainly didn't want it smothered in cocoa!

On the second occasion we used the rabbit, incidentally, our presenter was supposed to get up from the log where he had been sitting at the end of the show and walk off stage stroking the animal as the credits began to roll.

But he never moved, and wrapped up the programme from where he was sitting.

It was only after we had finished recording and he did stand up that we saw the reason. The rabbit had obviously ignored the first rule of television – always go to the toilet before going on set.

And it had emptied the entire contents of its bladder all over our unfortunate presenter!

But perhaps the most bizarre example of following the script to the letter came during the programme in which we featured the story of *Cinderella*.

At the end of the show, our presenter was to jump from a stile and stub his toe on something half buried in the ground.

He would wonder if it could have been a glass slipper as in the story, but it would turn out to be just a muddy old wellington.

When we got into studio to start recording, in the middle of the set was a rather grubby upturned dinghy.

I asked the props man what that was doing there and he said it was merely following the script.

And he showed me the line.

Instead of the PA typing muddy old boot, she had typed muddy old boat. No one had even thought to query what possible connection there may have been between the story of *Cinderella* and a muddy old boat!

For the most part, the director accepted that what I had written would not only run to time, but that any business I had written into the show would actually work.

But on one series, I had a director who would not leave anything to chance.

He had previously worked on *World in Action*, and his last assignment had ended with him escaping from a war zone under fire.

Not surprisingly, he did not want to leave anything to chance, and before we went into studio on the morning of each recording session, he insisted on running through every bit of business to make sure it would work.

He used to stay at the Midland Hotel in Manchester, and it was there we would meet over breakfast to run through the programmes in studio that week.

And it was there that I met a chamber maid with the greatest presence of mind I have ever come across.

Two of the supporting characters in our show were two puppets – a slow-witted snail and a sharper worm. In each programme, their role was to get across a basic mathematical concept to our young viewers in a way that would amuse them and hold their attention.

This particular sequence called for the presenter to roll balls down a ramp into a bucket, for the snail to count. But before the balls reached the bottom of the ramp, the worm had nipped out and grabbed them. So when the snail came to count the balls... well I think you get the picture.

I was quite happy that there would be no problem, but the director took some convincing and wanted to be assured, as usual, that everything I had written into the show would work. So we ended up in his hotel room in the Midland Hotel where I was to reassure him that everything would in fact go according to plan. And the only way to convince him was to run the scene.

To do this, we had the headboard off the bed. The producer had taken on the role of the presenter, and was holding one end of the headboard up while rolling fruit down it towards the waste bin on the floor, while I, who had been allotted the demanding role of the cheeky, mischievous worm, was on my hands and knees grabbing the fruit before it could reach its intended destination.

It was at this point that the chamber maid came in. She took in the scene, which even to her eyes must have seemed odd, and with the greatest presence of mind I have ever seen, said:

'Oh, I'm sorry sir. I didn't realise you hadn't finished breakfast!'

37

MODERN TIMES

DURING MY WRITING career, I have seen many changes, not least in technology, which has advanced broadcasting and the communications industry generally way beyond anything we could have dreamed of when I took my first steps in the business.

When I started in newspapers, reporting was done with a notebook and pencil, using shorthand. Pictures were transmitted by wire machines that were kept going with spares from the war surplus shops.

When I did my first course in press photography, the camera seemed to be the size of a small suitcase. It had a detachable flash gun that used bulbs resembling a miniature weather balloon. Film came on either glass plates or in sheets – difficult to imagine today in our digital world. I recall going on one of the first courses to be offered in this country in colour photography.

Television has seen even greater strides.

The studio cameras used to be the size of a modest wardrobe on wheels. Movement was very much restricted. The use of outside filming was minimal. It was expensive and there was a marked difference in quality between a film scene and a studio shot.

Eventually, equipment became smaller, lighter and more versatile. With improved technology and the advent of the portable video camera, it became as easy to shoot on location as it was to shoot in studio, with no difference in quality. While computer graphics have opened up a totally different world of animated entertainment.

All these changes have impacted enormously on the roles of writers, artistes, directors and technicians alike. They have given much more flexibility and cut down enormously on the need to build expensive sets. They have provided the means for making drama so much more gritty and realistic, and opened up a new, exciting, ever-changing and challenging future for all who work in the entertainment industry.

And no doubt in years to come there will be equally stunning changes in technology and techniques which will make today's methods look positively prehistoric.

At the peak of my career, the many regional ITV contractors in the UK were flourishing and commissioning their own programmes. If an idea didn't spark with one company, there was always another to try it on.

All that has changed now. The structure of ITV has changed as broadcasting has moved with the times. For television audiences, there are no longer only BBC 1, BBC 2 and ITV to choose from. The number of channels just goes on growing.

These days there are numerous reality TV shows, quizzes and game shows. It has become increasingly apparent that the public are more than willing and able to entertain themselves, and there is no shortage of folk desperate to get on television to showcase their talents.

The situation today encourages many more folk, particularly youngsters, to practice, develop and enjoy their particular talent, whether it be singing, dancing, instrumental, drama or stand-up comedy.

There are so many venues from school gigs to bars, social clubs, amateur dramatic and operatic societies where they can perform, many moving into the ranks of the professionals. If one day stardom beckons, so be it.

But the most important thing is that they have the opportunity and encouragement to enjoy what they are doing, at whatever level.

Although the face of television broadcasting has changed so dramatically over the past 20 years or so, the writing opportunities are still there. There are many companies producing an increasingly wide range of quality drama of all genre.

I am often asked for advice on writing for television, in particular the best way to start. And I find the best advice I can give is to recall my own tentative first steps into the business.

Writing for drama serials or series is as good a way as any to learn about the craft of writing for television. Working to deadlines; operating under pressure; writing initially for established characters then progressing to the development and introduction of new ones.

There are many drama serials and series which have a regular, steady, year-round output and a continuing need for storyline and script writers of quality. But I would stress the word quality.

The top three drama serials are obviously *Coronation Street*, *Emmerdale*, and *Eastenders,* but there are many more, and the fact that they are regularly the most watched programmes on TV only serves to emphasise just how high the standards of writing, acting and every aspect of production are.

But it is possible to do exactly what I did when I started out – to study the show, analyse it, become familiar with the locations, and most importantly get to know the characters as well as you know your own family. You must be able to come up with original thoughts, write convincing dialogue for your chosen characters. And before submitting a script, learn how to lay it out properly.

If your characters are believable, the words leap off the page and your trial script has a professional look about it, it will at least have a fair chance of being read by someone in the production office.

And of course there is radio. There are many opportunities for writers with something original and thought-provoking to say. Radio has always been a favourite medium for me as it has been for so many of my contemporaries. There is so much freedom without having to think of expensive budgets. Almost any effect can be created with sound.

It isn't easy. It requires a lot of dedication and hard work. And a good starting point, as with television scripts, is to familiarise yourself with any particular genre in which you may be interested.

Familiarise yourself with the time slots, programme content, length, and time of the day the drama is being transmitted. Knowing the audience you are writing for is very important, as it is with any script before putting pen to paper.

But no matter how much preparation you do, how much you craft and polish your work, you may still need a certain amount of luck – such as your efforts landing on the right desk at the right time.

Some years ago, I wrote my first *Saturday Night Theatre* play – and 90 minutes of radio is a lot of work, believe me.

It was a thriller, and full of optimism, as ever, I sent off my finished script to Alfred Bradley, who was the radio drama supremo at the BBC in Manchester.

He liked the play, and in keeping with the system in operation at the time, he put it up to London as one of his offerings for *Saturday Night Theatre.*

Unfortunately, London didn't share his enthusiasm, and the play came back.

I put it in a drawer, and forgot about it. If you couldn't sell a radio play to the BBC there was nowhere else to go.

Some 18 months later, I read it again and thought it was too good to stay buried for ever, so I re-worked it as a six-part drama serial and this time sent it direct to London.

Back came the reply that they were over-subscribed for 30 minute serials. But they liked it sufficiently to suggest that I try it as a *Saturday Night Theatre!*

So I took out the original, sent it off to London – and they bought it!

The lesson to be learned from this is that if at the first attempt your work doesn't land on the right desk at the right time – try, try and try again.

I never forget the words of a dear former colleague of mine on the Northern drama scene, sadly no longer with us. His name was Henry Livings and whenever he met anyone who said to him 'You are lucky to be a writer', he used to tell them that it was no coincidence that the luckiest people in this world, no matter what job they do, always seem to be the ones who work at it the hardest.

Henry was passionate about his work and his roots in the North of England. He was a fine actor and writer who did much to shape the television drama scene in the north of England, particular through a BBC North programme, *Northern Drift*.

He was passionate, too, about the theatre and after the Opera House in Manchester had been turned over to bingo, and the Palace Theatre had been closed for some time, he used his influence as a strong supporter of the Writers' Guild to rally every trade union representative in the entertainment business in the north of England, from Equity to the various technicians unions, to make their voices heard, to pile the pressure on anyone he felt may be able to help the cause, to bring about a re-opening of at least one of the venues.

His efforts didn't fall on deaf ears. The pressure yielded positive results, and both theatres were eventually re-furbished and re-opened to serve the theatregoers of Manchester once again as they had been built to do in the first place. And it is a fitting tribute to the hard work put in by Henry and his committee, of which I was proud to be a member, that both theatres are still open today.

Henry Livings was one more character in the northern entertainment scene who I was privileged to have known and to have worked with.

Whether you sell any of your work or not, the most important thing about the whole business of writing is that you enjoy it.

When you wake up every day and all you want to do is write, that is when you can truly call yourself a writer.

It is the same with actors. Many young drama school graduates have asked me for advice on how to get started in the business. I tell them to send pictures and a cv to the TV casting directors by all means, but as with writing, it is important to do what you seriously want to do. To act. There are many opportunities, whether it be with theatre workshop, rep company or amateur dramatic society. If the chance of a TV role comes up, be ready to seize the opportunity. But never let that dream make you lose sight of the fact that first and foremost you are an actor.

I could never understand why folk could be interested in what I was up to, why the first thing anyone would say to me on meeting was: 'And what are you working on at the moment?'

You wouldn't say that to a plumber, would you?

'What are you working on at the moment?'.

'I'm just putting a new boiler in for Mrs Gaskell. And Mrs Broadbottom has asked me to quote for changing the taps in her bathroom.'

I, like many of my contemporaries, was reluctant to say what we were working on, not so much because of the fear of giving away a good idea or plot line, but more because of a superstition that to tell anyone would be the kiss of death to the project.

But one thing a writer would rarely admit to is being out of work.

In the same way that we don't have debt any more, we have negative equity, the writer would merely be going through a period of negative employment. What the actors call 'resting'. Not that he would tell you in so many words.

But there are a number of giveaway signs – anything couched in vagueness is often the best pointer.

If a writer tells you dismissively that he is working on some unspecified project for some independent producer you have never heard of, it usually means he is spending much of his time contemplating his navel.

If he tells you dismissively without going into detail that he has just finished a book he has had on the go for the past couple of years, the assumption you can usually draw from that is that he is a slow reader.

He may tell you he has just finished a film, about details of which he is equally vague. Chances are he will be returning the DVD tomorrow.

So what am I doing at the moment?

I have just signed a two year contract with a major TV company – and if I don't keep up the payments, the set goes back!

38

CAN YOU HEAR ME AT THE BACK?

(Yes, but I'll be happy to change places with someone who can't!)

ONE OF THE rewards of being a writer is the opportunity to talk about your work to a variety of audiences should you feel so inclined, particular when you work for a show as well-known as *Coronation Street*.

And over the years, there have been many requests to talk to a range of audiences about my work from cruises and corporate conferences to WIs and Townswomen's Guilds.

I say a range of audiences because in my personal experience at one end of the scale I have spoken on the QE2 and entertained an audience of close on 800 at London University, while at the other end, I found myself talking to an audience of six at a retirement home in Manchester.

London University came about when I was working for an agent who provided speakers to universities for educational purposes. He would put on a day-long event at which a number of writers each did a half hour presentation. It ran from half past nine in the morning to five in the evening, the notion being that students could dip in and out of the event as they wished when something of interest came up.

I was amazed to find the theatre full as I took my place on stage, and I couldn't help wondering if it was because it was lunchtime and the students didn't have anywhere else to go. Or, more likely, the fact that I was following Colin Dexter, creator of *Inspector Morse!*

The audience of six came about when I was asked if I would go along to talk to the residents of a sizeable retirement home, which was a particularly inviting prospect at the time as I had a recently-published book to sell.

The retirement home was a good venue because the audience didn't have to catch a bus or drive home afterwards – an important factor when it came to book sales, as I found out in my early days of evening speaking events. It seemed that the dear ladies never carried money when they went out at night. At least, that's what they told me. Whether it was true or not, it did absolutely nothing for book sales!

When I turned up at the retirement home, there were notices all over the place proclaiming my attendance, and I went into the lounge where I was due to speak full of anticipation of a good evening.

Ten minutes after the appointed time for me to start – that was ten minutes after that night's episode of *Coronation Street* had finished – there was still no sign of anyone. Eventually, an elderly lady wandered in, swathed in dressing gown, slippers and sniffling into a handkerchief. She introduced herself as the organiser of the evening, then apologised profusely because the home had been hit by a flu virus. She didn't know how many would turn up, if any.

Eventually, I had six ladies including the organiser in front of me. One had to stand propped up against an armchair because she had just had a new knee, another one was deaf and a friend of hers had problems with her vision.

Six or six hundred, the show had to go on, and as I started to speak I felt it was going to be a long evening. It turned out to be longer than I could have imagined. My talk was punctuated from beginning to end by calls of 'What did he say?' by the lady who was hard of hearing, and 'Who is it?' by the lady who couldn't see.

I didn't have the heart to take a fee. I settled for a cup of tea instead, and an apology that they didn't have any biscuits because they hadn't been able to get to the shops!

By far the most satisfying and rewarding speaking 'jobs' for me and my wife, Avril, have been on cruise ships. It started a couple of years before I finished writing for *Coronation Street* when I first spoke on the QE2 about the show and my role as a writer.

When I had finished speaking, a lady came to join us and asked if Avril would take a photograph of her and myself together, which she did and we thought no more of it.

When I next spoke on the QE2 the following year, I was also doing a book signing when one lady I was signing for asked if I remembered her. It was the lady who had wanted her photograph taken with me the year before. She had seen my name in the advanced publicity for the cruise, and booked on it just to meet up with Avril and myself again.

The lady's name was Betty, she lived in Scunthorpe and we exchanged letters every month for close on twenty years after that. While we never met up again, we felt we knew her like a member of our own family.

After I finished writing for *Corrie* I went on to speak on a number of cruise ships, widening my programme to include much of the content of this book – not only my involvement with the world's most popular drama serial, but my love of the variety and rep scene and the unforgettable folk I had the privilege of knowing.

Each day I entertained the audience was on a sea day, when I quickly had to find my sea legs. On days when the weather was to say the least inclement, while the audience was sitting comfortably in finely upholstered chairs, it wasn't unusual for the lecturer to find himself on his feet in the lounge at the front or back of the ship tottering about like the proverbial drunken sailor.

I would speak for some forty five minutes then allow ten minutes or so for questions and discussion. Usually at the end of my talk I may have to field the occasional question, but by and large, not a lot. Then as soon as the theatre began to empty, folk would come down to the front and be queuing up with their questions, always starting off with 'I just wanted to ask, but I didn't like to in front of a room full of people.' The discussion would often go on all the way back to the bar or the dining room.

Once you have spoken on a cruise ship, nearly everyone knows you and for the rest of the trip you are public property. Passengers join you for coffee, for a pre-dinner drink, on a coach tour, eager to talk about the good old days of rep theatres, variety or *Coronation Street*.

The fund of stories they were able to add to my own recollections was endless, and they would like nothing better than to hear me recall one of their tales at a subsequent lecture, crediting them for bringing it up.

Which usually only served to encourage other passengers to come up with their own personal memories of the stars.

Then there were folk who would join me to tell me they knew me from somewhere, came from the same town or had worked for the same company I had worked for at some time.

I was lecturing on one cruise, when a lady came up to me to tell me I was the spitting image of someone she had seen in her village. I asked her where she came from and as it was the same village as I did, I told her it was probably me she had seen. But she would have none of it. It definitely wasn't me. But I was like him, she'd give me that.

She wasn't even convinced when I bumped into her back home. She just told me that she had been on a cruise where she had met someone who looked exactly like me!

39

AND THE SHOW GOES ON

OVER THE YEARS, many people have asked me to define what I see as the reason for the ongoing success of *Coronation Street*. Why does it have the same impact on viewers today as it did in that first episode over half a century ago?

Perhaps the most effective way to answer that is to go back to the very beginning. Why did the show have such a huge impact in the first place? As I stated earlier, Tony Warren got the formula exactly right when he created *Coronation Street* – his characters were finely drawn, viewers could instantly identify with them, the setting and situations were realistic, the writing, acting and production values were to the highest standard.

While technology has advanced enormously, none of these standards have changed, nor has the basic premise of the drama being about real life, real people in very real situations. What has changed over the years are the characters and the situations they experience on screen, the way they face up to each challenge and the way they react. They have constantly evolved, keeping pace with the rest of society as we have progressed over the years into the 21st century, reflecting changes in attitudes, behaviour patterns and relationships.

Just as they have done for over half a century, the characters and situations reach out to draw in the audience, to involve the viewers in their complicated lives, their triumphs, their tragedies. Some viewers may see them as an extension to their own families, their own lives. Others may just feel relieved that they don't know anyone quite like some of them.

One actor used to cross the threshold into the Granada TV studios and proclaim 'Goodbye, real world.'

But for millions of people, *Coronation Street* <u>is</u> the real world. The characters really exist to them. They share their lives. They worry about them. They love them. They hate them. They despair of them. But above all, like them or loathe them, they can't ignore them.

These days, you can rarely turn on the TV without being submerged in some form of reality show or other, whether it be quiz show, game show, chat show, or someone teaching us to dance, cook, eat, or sleep.

In modern television programme schedules, *Coronation Street* shines out like a beacon, its continuing popularity borne out by the number of nominations and awards it picks up year on year.

One of the most coveted of awards for me was always the National Television Award for best continuing drama serial, which was no stranger to our proud collection of annual achievements.

This award is voted for by the viewers, which says it all. They are the ones for whom we have been making the programme for all these years. Whenever I was asked who I thought was the most important character in *Coronation Street* I would say without hesitation 'You. The viewer. Because without you there would be no programme.'

I feel very proud and privileged to have been part of such a great television institution for so long.

Proud to have made my contribution to bringing drama, conflict, pathos and humour into the lives of so many viewers, young and old alike, for over a quarter of a century.

To have touched the hearts and minds of so many viewers, not only here at home but all over the world.

So how long can it go on?

I think the best way of answering that is to quote Harry Kershaw, one of the pioneers and all-time stalwarts of *Coronation Street*, when he was asked the same question.

There used to be a programme on Granada TV called *All Our Yesterdays* in which clips of programmes first aired 25 years earlier were shown.

When Harry was asked how long *Coronation Street* could go on, he would reply:

'For as long as life itself.'

Then after a moment's thought, he would add:

'And then for another 25 years on *All Our Yesterdays!*'

Lightning Source UK Ltd.
Milton Keynes UK
UKOW04f0310141214

243061UK00001B/1/P